W9-ABA-095

THE JUDGE
AND
THE HISTORIAN

THE JUDGE
AND
THE HISTORIAN

Marginal Notes on a
Late-Twentieth-Century
Miscarriage of Justice

◆

CARLO GINZBURG

Translated by
ANTONY SHUGAAR

VERSO
London • New York

First published by Verso 1999
This edition © Verso 1999
Translation © Antony Shugaar 1999
First published as *Il giudice e lo storico*
© Giulio Einaudi editore s.p.a. 1991
Revised edition first published as *Le juge et l'historien*
© Editions Verdier 1997

First paperback edition published by Verso 2002

All rights reserved

10 9 8 7 6 5 4 3 2 1

The moral rights of the author and translator have been asserted

Verso
UK: 6 Meard Street, London W1F 0EG
US: 180 Varick Street, New York, NY 10014–4606

Verso is the imprint of New Left Books

ISBN 1–85984–371–9

British Library Cataloguing in Publication Data
A catalogue record for this book is available from the British Library

Library of Congress Cataloging-in-Publication Data
A catalog record for this book is available from the Library of Congress

Typeset in Cochin by SetSystems Ltd, Saffron Walden, Essex
Printed and bound in the USA by R.R. Donnelly & Sons

CONTENTS

TRANSLATOR'S NOTE

This is a story of some complexity, spanning thirty years and, at times, evoking inquisitions stretching back four centuries.

At the centre of the story is a trial which reveals the workings of a perverse legal system and leads to a striking miscarriage of justice, whose victims are still in jail. Besides translating this book, I attended the trial in question as a reporter, and did my best to understand what was happening in the intricate and frenzied confusion surrounding it. But much escaped me.

Carlo Ginzburg's powerful analysis of the trial in question was first published in 1991, though this translation is based on the revised edition which appeared in French in 1997.

The book you are about to read stems from the events surrounding the death of Giuseppe Pinelli in December 1969, events which furnished the subject of Dario Fo's play *Accidental Death of an Anarchist*.

Pinelli died just before Christmas 1969, almost thirty years ago. In Italy, 1969 was a year marked by great labour unrest and massive left-wing demonstrations – it was also a time of sabre-rattling on the Right. Strikes, riots and dark hints of neo-Fascist *coups d'état* all crowded the scene during the 'hot autumn', as the latter part of 1969 came to be known.

On the afternoon of Friday 12 December 1969, a massive bomb blast had ripped through a farmers' bank in Milan. Friday afternoon was a busy time for the Banca Nazionale d'Agricoltura in Piazza Fontana; it was crowded with soberly dressed Lombard farmers making deposits at the end of the working week. One sight that remained indelibly stamped on the memories of witnesses was the array of dark, dusty, ownerless hats, piled on a counter in the bank. Nearly a hundred were injured; seventeen were killed.

According to one investigation of the events that followed the bombing, the judge who later conducted the preliminary inquest into the matter said, upon hearing the blast from his office in the Milan hall of justice, less than a mile from the site of the bombing, 'No, I don't think that was a boiler exploding. I think that was a bomb, and it sounded to me like an anarchist bombing.'

The story may be apocryphal, but within hours of the bombing, two anarchists had been arrested – anarchists who were later shown to have had nothing to do with it at all. In fact, it became clear in time that the bombing was a neo-Nazi terror attack, intended to destabilize Italy, making it ripe for a right-wing coup.

The two anarchists, however, were the first suspects. One was held and eventually tried; he was later freed, but not before spending years in prison. The other – Giuseppe Pinelli, a railway worker, a husband, and a father – was held (in violation of Italian law) for three days, and questioned exhaustively. At the end of the three days, he fell from a high window in the Milan police headquarters to the pavement below. He died on the way to hospital.

It has never been determined just how and why Pinelli fell out of that window. It was instantly perceived, however, throughout an angry and insurgent left-wing Italy, that Pinelli had been killed during a police interrogation, that the police were covering up his murder, and that one policeman in particular, Superintendent Luigi Calabresi, was responsible for that murder. Calabresi had been in charge of the interrogation. It was out of the window in Calabresi's office that Pinelli fell – or was thrown; it was Calabresi whom Licia Pinelli sued for her husband's wrongful death a year later.

The trial was never completed; in May 1972 Luigi Calabresi was shot twice and killed in front of his home, as he left for work one morning.

Calabresi's death – whoever may have been responsible for it – was perceived by the judicial authorities as the first in a series of political assassinations and other acts of violence (most famously, 'kneecapping'), a crescendo that culminated in the kidnap and murder of former Prime Minister Aldo Moro in 1978, and the kidnap – and successful rescue – of American general James Dozier in 1981. The 'years of lead', as they were dubbed by the Italian press, in a typically high-flown classical reference (the references are to Hesiod's 'age of lead', and to the hail of bullets that took nearly five hundred lives), lasted for roughly a decade, until the early 1980s.

An increasingly aggressive Italian judiciary and law enforcement managed to defeat the Red Brigades and other terrorist organizations in the years that followed, in part through the innovative evidentiary tool of the *pentito*, a repentant and confessed criminal turned state's witness.

One of the first of the *pentiti* was Patrizio Peci, a turncoat member of the Red Brigades; the history of atrocities that accompanies the use of *pentiti* began with Peci. The Red Brigades kidnapped Peci's younger brother, Cristoforo, and sent the police a video of Cristoforo's execution – a single bullet to the side of the head.

The use of *pentiti* continued, against terrorists and then against the Mafia. They were effective – about that there was no doubt. Still, there was a pact-with-the-Devil quality to *pentiti*, increasingly evident with the Mafiosi turncoats who, alone, allowed the judiciary to dismantle large sections of organized crime in Italy.

This surely shows the importance of the principle that only democratic justice could effectively combat the Mafia; that it was the absence of the principle of justice that allowed the Mafia to flourish. One might cite the effective – if heavy-handed – elimination of the Mafia under Mussolini's appointed delegate to Sicily, the Prefetto Mori, and its immediate and complete return following the American liberation.

The dangers of the *pentiti* are clearly illustrated in this book; the prosecution and conviction of Adriano Sofri, Ovidio Bompressi and Giorgio Pietrostefani are clearly the product of a system of justice willing to condemn on the flimsiest tissue of testimony.

I saw the imposing hall of justice in Milan where this trial took place, built during the Fascist regime. I watched Calabresi's family – his widow, his two sons, now adults – as they attended the trial. I saw Prosecuting Magistrate Ferdinando Pomarici, clearly a man out to win, even if the result was a mockery of justice.

Until I read this book, however, I had no real idea of what

had happened in that courtroom. Ginzburg's lucid yet passionate analysis made it possible for me to see – in hindsight – how little I had grasped of the astonishing miscarriage that has stained the record of Italian justice. It will, I am sure, afford similar illumination to others.

Antony Shugaar
New York City, December 1998

Addendum by Carlo Ginzburg

A note on the latest developments: as this English translation goes to press (December 1998), the Brescia Court of Appeal is preparing to issue yet another verdict in the succession of contradictory judgements in this seemingly endless case. This comes on the heels of a verdict by the Milan Court of Appeal rejecting a request by the lawyers for Sofri, Bompressi and Pietrostefani for a new trial on the basis of new evidence; that verdict rejecting the request for a new trial was, in its turn, annulled by the Italian Supreme Court (or Corte di Cassazione). The Brescia Court of Appeal now faces two possibilities. It can either (1) decide to order a new trial; or (2) reject that request, leaving the three men in prison. To take the latter course of action would seem to go against the spirit of the verdict of the Italian Supreme Court, mentioned above. But to make predictions in accordance with a sense of justice (or even common sense) would be, in a case of this sort, quite a risk.

Carlo Ginzburg
Bologna, December 1998

P.S. My final remark proved to be unfortunately appropriate. On 1 March 1999 the Brescia Court of Appeal rejected the request for a new trial, claiming that the new evidence was insufficient. An appeal against the rejection has been submitted to the Supreme Court (Corte di Cassazione): the latest episode, so far, of this endless legal story.

March 1999

I would like to thank Paolo Carignani, Luigi Ferrajoli and Adriano Prosperi for their comments.

THE JUDGE
AND
THE HISTORIAN

INTRODUCTION

I have written this book for two reasons. The first is personal. I have known Adriano Sofri for more than thirty years. He is one of my closest friends. In summer 1988, he was accused of ordering one man to kill another. I am certain that this accusation is groundless. The Milan Court of Assizes, however, found otherwise. On 2 May 1990, that court sentenced Adriano Sofri (along with Giorgio Pietrostefani and Ovidio Bompressi) to twenty-two years in prison, and Leonardo Marino (their accuser) to eleven years. The first two (Sofri and Pietrostefani) for ordering the murder of police superintendent Luigi Calabresi; the other two (Bompressi and Marino), respectively, for actually committing the murder – in Milan, on 17 May 1972 – and as an accomplice.

According to Italian law, the accused must be considered innocent until the verdict is confirmed by the highest court of appeal in Italy. At the beginning of the first criminal trial, however, Adriano Sofri publicly declared that he would under no circumstances avail himself of his right to appeal against the court's judgement. I – like many others – immediately questioned the wisdom of this decision, though not the sincerity of the reasoning behind it. Over the last several years in Italy, verdicts in trials for political crimes and Mafia-linked crimes have often (extremely often, in fact) been overturned on appeal, or in the Italian Supreme Court. By giving up – in advance – his right to appeal, Sofri wished to avoid an acquittal deferred. He felt, rightly or wrongly, that such an acquittal would be less complete, less clear – almost darkened by a stain. There were those who considered his decision to be an unjustified form of pressure on the judges presiding over the lower-court trial. Those who know Sofri well, on the other hand, saw in this decision a distinct personality trait: an elevated self-image, the certainty of his own innocence, and an intolerance of compromise. By deciding to renounce his right to appeal, he has lost the right to defend his innocence in the trial about to be held in a higher court.

I am writing on the eve of the second trial, prompted by the pain caused by an unjust conviction weighing on my friend, and by my wish to persuade others of his innocence. The form this book has taken, however (quite distant, as we shall see, from a personal testimony), has a different provenance. And that brings me to the second of the two reasons – mentioned above – for writing this book.

The transcripts of the trial in Milan and the judicial investigation that led up to that trial have repeatedly brought me face to face with the relationship, so intricate and ambiguous, between judges and historians. This topic has interested me for years. In a number of essays, I have attempted to explore the implications – both methodological and (in a broader sense) political – of a series of features common to both professions: evidence, proof, and testimony.[1] The time has surely come for a more thorough examination. This takes its place in a venerable tradition – the title itself (fairly obvious, for that matter) of this short book mirrors, as I discovered while writing it, the title of an essay published in 1939 by Piero Calamandrei.[2] Today, however, the dialogue between historians and judges – never a smooth one – has taken on a crucial importance for both. I will try to explain why, starting with a specific and concrete case – one which, for the reasons explained above, touches me personally.

Bologna, summer/autumn 1990

The written judgement was published, after an appalling delay, on 12 January 1991. It is analysed in the second part of this book. I have decided to maintain a distinction between the two sections, for reasons I will explain below.

Los Angeles, February 1991

I

A slight sense of disorientation. That is the first impression that comes when someone – accustomed for professional reasons to reading the transcripts of sixteenth- and seventeenth-century trials of the Inquisition – sets out to read the proceedings of the preliminary judicial investigation carried out in 1988 by Antonio Lombardi (investigating magistrate) and Ferdinando Pomarici (assistant district attorney) against Leonardo Marino and his alleged accomplices. Disorientation, because these documents have, against all expectations, a curiously familiar appearance. There are important differences, such as the presence of attorneys for the defence (even though a manual of the Inquisition, such as 'Sacro Arsenale' by Eliseo Masini (Genoa, 1621) does indeed suggest that defence attorneys should be provided, they rarely were at the time). None the less, much as in the halls of inquisitorial justice three or four centuries ago, the interrogations of those accused of a crime take place in secret, far from the prying gaze of the public (at times, even in such inappropriate locations as *carabinieri* barracks).

They take place – or rather, they took place. With the approval of the new penal code, the seal of secrecy covering preliminary investigations has partially disappeared and, with it, the inquisitorial aspect that was so difficult to reconcile with the other, largely accusatory aspect of courtroom hearings.[3] The preliminary investigation of Marino and his alleged confederates carried out by Lombardi and Pomarici was one of the last (perhaps the very last) to fall under the old Italian penal code.

The impression of continuity with the past which so struck

me immediately, however, was not only a product of the institutional aspects of the preliminary investigation. That impression was created by a more subtle and specific resemblance to the trials of the Inquisition that I know best – the trials of men and women accused of witchcraft. In those trials, accusations levelled by accomplices were fundamental – especially when the confessions of the accused tended to revolve around the Black Sabbath, a night-time gathering of witches and sorcerers.[4] In some cases spontaneously, but more often urged on by torture or the judges' guidance, the accused would ultimately yield up the names of those who had taken part in the diabolical rites with them. In this way, a trial could (and often did) give rise to five, ten, or twenty others, in the end ensnaring entire communities in their coils. The Roman Inquisition, however, heir to the Inquisition of the Middle Ages (or, as it was also called, the episcopal Inquisition), while encouraging the persecution of witchcraft, was also the source of the earliest doubts concerning the juridical legitimacy of such proceedings. At the beginning of the seventeenth century, in the context of the Roman Congregation of the Holy Office, a document was drawn up, entitled *Instructio pro formandis processibus in causis strigum, sortilegiorum & maleficiorum* (Instructions Concerning the Best Way to Proceed in the Trials of Witches, Sorcerers and Evil-Doers); this document marked a sharp break with the past. Experience – according to the document – showed that to date, trials for witchcraft had almost never been carried out on the basis of acceptable criteria.[5] The judges of the outlying inquisitorial courts were therefore duly advised that they should make use of 'exquisite diligenze giuditiali' (extreme judicial care) and verify all the declarations of the accused; they should track down, if possible, the *corpus delicti*; they should seek proof that a cure or an illness could not be attributed to natural causes.

Similarly, the trial I wish to explore here revolves around a figure who is both accused and witness, a defendant accusing both himself and others. The self-accusations of Leonardo Marino are the culmination of a tragic sequence of notorious events. Let me recall them briefly. On 12 December 1969, at the height of a period of strikes and labour conflict dubbed the 'hot autumn', a bomb went off in Milan in a branch of a farmers' bank, the Banca dell'Agricoltura, killing sixteen people (another person died shortly thereafter) and injuring eighty-eight others. Two days later, the police arrested an anarchist named Pietro Valpreda; the moderate press (first and foremost, the *Corriere della Sera*) described him as the bomber. Another anarchist, Giuseppe (Pino) Pinelli, employed by the state railway, was summoned to police headquarters for questioning. Three nights went by, and Pinelli's body fell from the window of the office of Superintendent Luigi Calabresi; in the office at the time were an officer of the *carabinieri* and four policemen. A journalist found Pinelli unconscious on the pavement. Two hours later, at a hastily convened press conference, Milan's chief of police, Marcello Guida, informed the press that Pinelli – after being confronted with irrefutable evidence of his complicity in the bombing carried out by Valpreda – had leapt from the window, crying: 'This is the end of anarchy.' This version was subsequently abandoned. The new version stated that Pinelli, during a break in questioning, went over to the window to smoke a cigarette; he fainted and fell out. These two conflicting versions were soon joined by a third, which began to circulate insistently among the Italian left wing (parliamentary and non-parliamentary): Pinelli, killed by a karate chop from a policeman, was already dead when he was tossed out of Calabresi's office window. In 1969 the leftist group Lotta Continua began a violent campaign in its various publications against Calabresi, the police superintendent who had been questioning Pinelli. Calabresi, according to this campaign, had murdered Pinelli.

After a few months, Calabresi sued the daily newspaper *Lotta Continua* for libel. During the ensuing trial, on 22 October 1971, the court ordered Pinelli's corpse to be exhumed. Shortly thereafter, Calabresi's lawyer challenged the presiding judge – a retrial was ordered. On 17 May 1972 Calabresi was shot twice and killed outside the main entrance of his apartment building. No one claimed responsibility for the assassination. The following day, a note in the daily paper *Lotta Continua* basically approved of the murder ('a deed in which the exploited recognize their own yearning for justice') but took no responsibility for it. Some time later, a number of right-wing extremists were indicted for the crime; proceedings were suspended due to lack of evidence. Sixteen years went by. On 19 July 1988 a former Fiat factory worker, Leonardo Marino, who had been a Lotta Continua militant, entered the *carabinieri* office in Ameglia (a small town not far from Bocca di Magra, where Marino was living with his family) and declared that he was haunted by guilt and wished to confess to a series of crimes bound up with his history as a political militant. (The account of Marino's confession given here is the one initially reported, not the version that emerged two years later, during the trial.) On 20 July, Marino was taken to the offices of the Nucleo

Operativo (Operations Command Centre) of the Milan *cara-binieri*, where transcripts of his first statements were made. The following day, in the presence of an assistant prosecuting attorney, Ferdinando Pomarici, Marino confessed that he had taken part in the assassination of Calabresi, as well as in a series of robberies between 1971 and 1987. The assassination had been ordered (again, according to Marino) by a majority vote of the national executive committee of Lotta Continua. Marino himself had been urged to participate in the killing by one of the leaders of Lotta Continua, Giorgio Pietrostefani; Marino had agreed to take part only after being given explicit assurance of the decision (in Pisa, following a rally) by Sofri, to whom Marino was particularly close. A few days after this meeting with Sofri, Marino had travelled to Milan and waited in front of Calabresi's apartment building with Ovidio Bompressi. Immediately after the shooting he had picked up Bompressi, the actual killer, in a car that had been stolen three days before, and fled. All of the above was recounted in great and plentiful detail. Still, the accounts of a defendant/witness, however detailed, are not sufficient proof – that had already been established by the magistrates of the Roman Inquisition in the early seventeenth century, as they reread the minutes of the witch-craft trials conducted by their fellow judges. For a confession to be considered reliable, it must be corroborated by objective evidence.

We shall soon see how the judges in the trial of the accused assassins of Luigi Calabresi dealt with this problem. We should point out immediately, however, that the search for objective evidence or proof is a pursuit shared not only by the inquisitors of 350 years ago and the judges of the present day, but by modern historians. Concerning this common territory, and especially concerning its implications, we would do well to meditate at greater length.

II

The ties between history and law have always been close – they date back two thousand five hundred years, to the emergence in Greece of the literary genre that we call 'history'. While the word 'history' [*historia*] derives from medical parlance, the reasoning skills it implies derive from the field of law. History as a specific intellectual activity was founded (as Arnaldo Momigliano noted some years ago) at the intersection of medicine and rhetoric: history examines cases and situations, seeking out their natural causes, in emulation of medicine; history then sets them forth in accordance with the rules of rhetoric, an art of persuasion that developed in the courtroom.[6]

In the classical tradition, what was expected of historical narrative (and, for that matter, of poetry) was, first of all, a quality that the Greeks called *enargeia*; the Romans termed it *evidentia in narratione*. These names described an ability to depict characters and situations vividly. Not unlike a lawyer, a historian should persuade through effective argumentation, capable even of conveying an illusion of reality, not through the adducing of evidence or the analysis of evidence adduced by others.[7] The production of evidence was an activity more properly suited to antiquarians or savants; until the second half of the eighteenth century, however, historians and antiquarians worked in totally independent fields of endeavour, which were generally pursued by different individuals.[8] When the Jesuit scholar Henri Griffet, in his treatise *Traité des différentes sortes de preuves qui servent à établir la vérité de l'histoire* (1769), compared the historian to a judge who carefully evaluates evidence and testimony, he was describing an approach that had not yet been taken, though it was probably widely advocated. It found application just a few years later in Edward Gibbon's *The Decline and Fall of the Roman Empire* (1776) – the first work that successfully combined history and antiquarianism.[9]

Comparison between historian and judge enjoyed great popularity. In a famous axiom, originally set forth by Schiller – *Die Weltgeschichte ist das Weltgericht* – Hegel condensed, in the twofold meaning of *Weltgericht* ('verdict of the world' or 'judgement of the world', but also 'Last Judgement'), the essence of his own philosophy of history: the secularization of the Christian vision of universal history, or history of the world [*Weltgeschichte*].[10] The accent fell on the verdict (with the ambiguity mentioned above): but it enjoined the historian to judge figures and events in accordance with a principle – the higher interests of the state – that was substantially alien to both justice and morality. In the passage from Griffet, on the other hand, the accent fell on what precedes the verdict – that is to say, the impartial evaluation of evidence and testimony on the part of the judge. At the end of the nineteenth century, Lord Acton, in the inaugural lecture delivered on the occasion of his appointment as Regius Professor of Modern History at Cambridge University (1895), insisted on both points: historiography, when it is based on documents, can rise above all disagreements and become an established court of law, the same for one and all.[11] These words reflected a tendency that was rapidly becoming widespread, encouraged by the prevailing climate of positivism. Between the end of the nineteenth century and the first few decades of the twentieth, historiography, especially political historiography – and, most particularly, the historiography of the French Revolution – took on a distinctly judicial appearance.[12] Given the tendency, however, to associate political passion closely with the professional duty of impartiality, a jaundiced eye of suspicion was turned upon those who – like Taine (who, for his part, boasted that he wished to engage in 'moral zoology') – examined the phenomenon of the Revolution with the attitude of a 'supreme and imperturbable judge'. Alphonse Aulard, whom I have just quoted, along with his academic adversary Albert Mathiez, preferred to don the garb of, variously – as the case suggested – prosecuting attorney or lawyer for the defence, in order to prove, with the use of richly detailed *dossiers*, Robespierre's misdeeds or Danton's corruption. This tradition of summations at once political and moral, followed by convictions or acquittals, enjoyed enormous longevity: *Un jury pour la Révolution*, by Jacques Godechot, one of the best-known living historians of the French Revolution, was published in 1974.[13]

The judicial model exerted two intertwining effects on historians. On the one hand, it encouraged them to focus their attention on events (political, military, diplomatic events) which could be ascribed, without excessive problems, to the actions of one or more individuals; on the other hand, it led them to avoid all phenomena (history of social groups, history of mentalities and attitudes, and so on) which did not lend themselves to this explicatory network. As if in a photographic negative, we can see – in inverted form – the orders of the day around which the journal *Annales d'histoire économique et sociale*, founded in 1929 by Marc Bloch and Lucien Lefebvre was established: a rejection of *histoire événementielle*, a desire to explore a more profound, less obvious type of history. It should come as no surprise to find, in the essay on method penned by Bloch just before his death, the ironic exclamation: 'Robespierrists, anti-Robespierrists, just do us a favour: for Heaven's sake, tell us simply who Robespierre was.' In the face of the dilemma 'judging or understanding' Bloch opted, without a moment's hesitation, for the second alternative.[14] This, as we find obvious nowadays, was the historiographical path destined to triumph. To remain in the context of studies of the French Revolution, Albert Mathiez's attempt to explain Danton's politics through his and his friends' corruption (*La corruption parlementaire sous la Terreur*, 1927) appears inadequate nowadays; while Georges Lefebvre's reconstruction of the Great Fear of 1789 (*La Grande Peur de 1789* [1932]) has become a classic of contemporary historiography.[15] Lefebvre was not a member of the *Annales* group in the narrow sense. Still, *The Great Fear* would never have been written had it not been for the precedent set by *Les Rois Thaumaturges* by Marc Bloch, Lefebvre's colleague at the University of Strasbourg.[16] Both books revolve around events that never occurred: the power to cure cases of scrofula attributed to the kings of France and England, and the attacks by bands of brigands in the service of the 'aristocratic conspiracy'. What made these phantasmagorical events historically significant was their symbolic efficacy – that is to say, the image they created in the minds of myriad nameless individuals. It would be difficult to imagine anything further from a moralistic historiography based upon a judicial model.

We should certainly rejoice over its diminished prestige, which declined with the dwindling of the image of the historian interpreting the higher interests of the state. While some twenty years ago, however, it might have been possible to adhere wholeheartedly to the sharp distinction between judge and historian set forth by Bloch, the matter appears far more complicated today. The proper and understandable intolerance of a historiography based upon a judicial model tends, increasingly, to extend even to that which originally justified the analogy between historian and judge already formulated by the Jesuit scholar Henri Griffet: the idea of proof. (What I am about to say brushes only tangentially upon matters as they stand in Italy. To paraphrase Brecht, we might say that the bad old things – beginning with the philosophy of Giovanni Gentile, still an invisible presence in the Italian cultural landscape – have protected us from the bad new things.[17])

For many historians, the notion of proof is out of fashion: like that of truth, to which it is bound by a very solid historical (and therefore unnecessary) link. There are many reasons for this devaluation, and not all of them are intellectual in nature. One reason certainly has to do with the overblown importance acquired – on both shores of the Atlantic, in France and in the United States – by the term 'representation'. Because of the various uses to which it has been put, the term winds up creating an insurmountable wall around the historian. Historical sources tend to be examined exclusively as sources of themselves (of the way in which they were constructed), not as sources of the things they discuss. In other words, there is an analysis of the sources (written, visual, and so on) as evidence of social 'representations': at the same time, there is a general rejection of the possibility of analysing the relationships between these representations and the reality they depict or represent; this is dismissed as an unforgivable instance of naive positivism.[18] Now, those relationships are never straightforward – to think that they are simple mirrorings of reality would indeed be naive. We know perfectly well that every representation is constructed in accordance with a predetermined code – to gain direct access to historical reality (or reality itself, for that matter) is impossible, by definition. To infer from this fact, however, that reality is unknowable is to fall into a lazily radical form of scepticism, at once unsustainable in existential terms and inconsistent in logical terms – as we know full well, the fundamental decision of the sceptic is not subjected to the methodological doubt he claims to profess.[19]

For me, and for many others, the notions of 'proof' and 'truth' are, rather, integral parts of the historian's profession. This does not mean, of course, that nonexistent phenomena or falsified documents are of little historical importance – Bloch and Lefebvre taught us the opposite long ago. Still, any analysis of representations cannot overlook the principle of reality. The nonexistence of the bands of brigands renders more significant (because more profound and revealing) the fear that spread among the French peasants in the summer of 1789. A historian has the right to detect a problem where a judge might find an 'absence of grounds for proceedings'. This is a major divergence which, however, presupposes an element that links, rather than divides, historians and judges: the use of proof. The professions of both historians and judges rest upon the possibility of proving, according to given rules, that x did y, where x may equally well indicate the protagonist (perhaps nameless) of a historic event or the subject of a penal proceeding; and *y* an action of any sort.[20]

Obtaining proof, however, is not always possible; and even when it is, the result will always be measurable in terms of probability (perhaps 99.9 per cent), not absolute certainty.[21] Here, a further divergence arises: one of the many that mark – beyond the initial similarities mentioned above – the profound distinction between historians and judges. Let me try to explore it as we move forward. At that point, the implications – and the limitations – will emerge in that intriguing analogy suggested by Luigi Ferrajoli: 'A trial is, so to speak, the only case of "historiographic experimentation" – in a trial the sources are forced to interact *de vivo*, not only because they are heard directly, but also because they are forced to confront one another, subjected to cross-examination and prompted to produce, as in a psychodrama, the adjudicated event.'[22]

III

I have consulted the records of one of these historiographical experiments: the transcripts of the interrogations conducted during the preliminary inquest by Judge Antonio Lombardi, the ordinance-sentence calling for a trial that Lombardi drew up, the transcripts of the hearings of the Milan Court of Assizes, with Judge Manlio Minale presiding, the summations of Assistant District Attorney Ferdinando Pomarici, the summations of the lawyers for the defence, along with various ancillary material concerning Leonardo Marino and his alleged confederates. In all, some three thousand pages. I have already spoken of the unexpected (and therefore disconcerting) sensation of familiarity that came over me as I read the testimony assembled by the investigating magistrate. Of course, this sensation dwindled considerably once I moved on to the transcripts of courtroom testimony. The exchanges between the various parties, continually filtered and mediated by the presiding judge, create an atmosphere that is entirely different from that of an Inquisition trial. Conversely (and paradoxically), the liveliness of the transcriptions from tape-recordings of courtroom hearings is far closer to the transcripts of the Inquisition than is the rigid bureaucratic language into which the interrogations of the preliminary inquest are transcribed (and distorted), even though the preliminary inquest is much closer, in juridical terms, to the trials of the Inquisition. Certainly, in either case, these are *transcriptions*: in the passage from spoken to written word, intonations, hesitations, silences and gestures are lost. They are lost, but not entirely. Often – unwittingly following in the footsteps of the notaries of the Holy Office – the court stenographers record, in parentheses, tears, laughter, failures to answer, or answers given with special passion.[23] Here, transcription is already interpretation, conditioning later interpretations undertaken in the near future (by this author, for instance) or the distant future.[24]

It never occurred to me that I might use this documentary material to reconstruct – from a historical point of view – the events that were being judged here. I did not wish to – and in any case, I would not have known how. My objectives were far more limited: an analysis of the court records, with a view to emphasizing the divergences and convergences between historian and judge. The convergences, as I have said, comprise especially the use of evidence. Unlike a judge, however (or an oral historian), I am not capable of taking part in the production of the sources I analyse. I can only – with the assistance, sometimes supportive, sometimes antagonistic, of those who have gone before me (judges, witnesses, defendants, stenographers) – participate in deciphering them.

'The confessions of Marino', wrote Investigating Magistrate Antonio Lombardi in his ordinance-sentence, in the chapter 'The Sources of Proof', 'constitute . . . in terms of quality and quantity, the dominant source of proof in this trial.' Their sincerity (the investigating magistrate explained) is unquestionable. In Marino's soul, an unbridled disgust for the crimes he had committed began to ferment. A profound ethical impulse drove him to denounce himself and his former comrades:

> For many years, the persuasion had been taking root within me, dictated by moral and religious feelings, that I should confess to the appropriate authorities concerning acts and circumstances in which I had been involved between the late sixties and the early seventies, when I was a militant in the extra-parliamentary movement 'Lotta Continua'. Even though I was certain that I could never come under suspicion, in part because I had never been in trouble with the law, for the past three to four years there had been welling up within me the need, the requirement, to come to terms with what I had done in a political context that I abandoned more than fifteen years ago. . . . Even though I may feel that many may look upon this statement with scepticism, I have decided to confess those things that I

have done and those about which I have knowledge, especially out of respect towards these boys [his two sons]. (*Inf. test.*, p. 1)[25]

The robberies in which he had taken part (at least those prior to 1976) had been undertaken – Marino said – by an illegal group within Lotta Continua, headed by Pietrostefani. As for the murder of Calabresi, that had been deliberated in a meeting of the executive committee of Lotta Continua, put to a vote, then approved by a majority. Behind the actual killers, the militants Bompressi and Marino, we begin to see the outlines of the instigators of the crime, two important leaders, Sofri and Pietrostefani, involving the highest levels of the organization. Calabresi, then, was killed – in the fullest sense of the term – by Lotta Continua.

The investigating magistrate, however, knew very well that the claimed sincerity of Marino's repentance is not sufficient to ensure the veracity of his confessions. 'They [his confessions] have often been found to be in agreement with testimony offered on the same point by witnesses and (in connection with important details) also by other defendants; they have also found unequivocal confirmation in investigations by the judicial police, on-site investigations, and ballistics tests.' Of course, the investigating magistrate continues:

not all of the statements are always circumstantiated and meticulous in their details; at times they are based on hearsay; minor errors, oversights, inaccuracies, overlapping recollections, are always inevitable in the reconstruction of so many events that happened so many years ago. . . . These minor errors, all the same, are, in the view of the Investigating Magistrate, more than outweighed by the careful verification of the references linked to the accusations of complicity. (*Ordinance-Sentence*, pp. 70–71)[26]

Here, the 'minor errors' appear as marginal obstacles, which are subsequently 'overcome'. Further on, they become a warrant of authenticity instead:

The evaluation of the accusation of complicity should ... be conducted in realistic terms; to expect that any account of a great many acts and circumstances should be absolutely free of errors or marginal inconsistencies would be tantamount to expecting superhuman abilities in the person recounting those acts and circumstances, in this case, Marino; Marino's account actually demonstrates its spontaneous and authentic nature through the existence of minor errors or marginal inconsistencies in the narration of things that happened so many years ago. The basic problem is to determine whether whatever minor errors or inconsistencies there may be in this account are such that they undermine the probative validity of the account taken as a whole. And this, in the view of the Investigating Magistrate, is decidedly not the case with the close-knit account of the defendant. (*Ordinance-Sentence*, pp. 91–2)

Let us now examine the 'minor errors' that – as Judge Lombardi recognizes in his ordinance-sentence – Marino committed in his account of the assassination of Calabresi.

(*a*) *The colour of the Fiat 125 that was stolen and then used in the assassination.* It was dark blue, not beige, as Marino claimed at first (he later said that he had mixed it up with a car he stole at Massa to carry out a robbery).

(*b*) *The route used to escape from the scene of the crime.* In the confession made during the preliminary inquest, Marino stated that he drove away from the Via Cherubini by taking the Via Giotto or the Via Belfiore towards the Piazza Wagner. Eyewitness accounts, on the other hand, have the killers driving away along the Via Cherubini, then turning into the Via Rasori, in the direction of the Via Ariosto at the corner of the Via Alberto da Giussano, where the killers abandoned the dark-blue Fiat 125 with its engine running. When Adriano Sofri pointed out this startling inconsistency during the preliminary inquest, the magistrates replied that Marino, who was not familiar with the names of the streets in Milan,[27] had described the escape route based on a street map that the prosecuting attorney had 'presented to him upside-down'. '[Marino]', we read in the ordinance-sentence, 'as he looked at the Via Cherubini the other way round, and indicated that he had immediately turned right, read the name of the Via Giotto or the Via Belfiore instead of the Via Rasori.' Now, the clumsy expression used by the investigating magistrates – 'presented to him upside-down' – is evidently meant to indicate that the street map was orientated at – from the point of view of the person using it (Marino) – south to north, rather than north to south. At this point, we may consider two hypotheses: Marino, in order to be able to read the street names, which were in fact written 'upside-down', asked the prosecuting attorney to turn the map so that it was orientated north to south, as is normal; or, unable to make out the names of the streets, he simply pointed out his route to the prosecuting attorney. In either case, the prosecuting attorney fails to notice that the route indicated by Marino is inconsistent not only with the eyewitness accounts, but even with the site on which the dark-blue Fiat 125 was actually found. In an effort to conceal their own sloppiness, the investigating magistrates not only pass the bungling defendant, but pass him with flying colours: 'In conclusion, Marino described perfectly the main escape route, and the subordinate escape route (which was actually used)' (*Preliminary Inquest*, p. 257).

Here, Marino's version was recognized as erroneous (albeit somewhat belatedly) by Judge Lombardi and by Assistant District Attorney Pomarici. There was no alternative: it is obvious that any description of the escape route would necessarily lead to the dark-blue Fiat 125 abandoned by the killers in the Via Ariosto on the corner of the Via Alberto da Giussano. Overall, however, the preliminary inquest offers a radically different evaluation of Marino's confession. In the chapter of the ordinance-sentence entitled 'Objective Corroboration', dedicated to the preparation and carrying out of the assassination of Calabresi, it says (page 264) that not only does Marino's account 'dovetail perfectly' with the police reconstruction, but it actually makes it possible to 'correct . . . some of its inaccuracies'. In other words, rather than trying to find objective corroboration for the defendant's confession, the preliminary inquest makes use of that confession as a touchstone with which to test (and, if necessary, discard) the eyewitness accounts.

I V

The presiding judge of the Milan Court of Assizes, Manlio Minale, made it clear from the very beginning of the trial that he was not about to place blind faith in the findings of the preliminary inquest conducted by Judge Antonio Lombardi and Assistant District Attorney Ferdinando Pomarici (the latter having overseen only the first four interrogations of Marino). Minale was determined to verify the defendant's credibility from top to bottom. Beginning with Marino's first testimony in court (9 January 1990), doubt was cast on the profound ethical foundation of his repentance. The presiding judge observed that just before Marino went to the parish priest of Bocca di Magra to speak of his remorse, he had committed another hold-up (*Trial*, p. 14). 'In other words – the presiding judge asked Marino at a certain point – if you had found the money, you would have continued the same sort of life, and you would have found some way of lulling your conscience, wouldn't you?' (*Trial*, p. 28). During testimony the following day (10 January 1990), Minale pointed out to Marino that in the preliminary inquest he had provided three different versions of the preparations leading up to the assassination of Calabresi. *First version*: Marino was approached repeatedly by Bompressi; he agreed to take part in the assassination, and he received from Sofri and Pietrostefani at Pisa (13 May 1972) confirmation of the

THE JUDGE AND THE HISTORIAN

decision taken by the executive committee. *Second version*: Marino received the first invitation to participate from Bompressi; he was given detailed instructions by Pietrostefani, and he resolved his last lingering doubts at Pisa in a meeting with Sofri, in which Pietrostefani also took part (*Trial*, pp. 39–42). *Third version*: the murder was planned in a series of discussions held by an unspecified 'group' (in Marino's response, he said the group comprised Pietrostefani, Bompressi, and himself). During the course of the trial, there emerged a fourth version, which eliminated Pietrostefani from the meeting at Pisa.[28] The reasons for Marino's last revision can easily be guessed at. During the preliminary inquest, Pietrostefani had pointed out that a man wanted by the police, as he was at the time, would be unlikely to show his face in Pisa, where he was exceedingly well known, especially on a day when the entire city was going to be heavily patrolled (Lotta Continua had organized a rally in commemoration of the late Franco Serantini, a young man who had died in prison, without medical care, just a few days before, as the result of a beating administered by the police during a demonstration). In that case, however – the presiding judge objected – why had Marino told the prosecuting attorney that Pietrostefani had participated 'either directly or from a distance' in the conversation in Pisa? Marino was visibly rattled:

> Well, look, I . . . when I made, let us say, this first statement, in which I spontaneously and impulsively declared that I had been approached by Pietrostefani and Sofri, I meant to say that I had spoken about this matter, first with one of them and later with the other. Clearly, I wasn't. . . .

That is to say, I thought that it was not important at that point to specify clearly with whom I had spoken first and with whom I spoke later, the places, and so on and so forth. Later, recalling more carefully.... In effect, at Pisa, I spoke only with Sofri, also because, in fact, let me repeat, I had had plenty of opportunities to speak with 'Pietro' [i.e. Pietrostefani] previously, and to discuss these matters with him already.... (10 January 1990; *Trial*, p. 71)

V

Marino speaks of an isolated mistake, committed 'spontaneously and impulsively'. Instead, this was just one of the many minor adjustments he introduced in the various versions of this crucial episode that he supplied, progressively, over the course of the trial.

Interrogation of 21 July 1988:

During this same period, Serantini died at Pisa, just a few days prior to the murder of Calabresi; I remember that there was a huge demonstration, in which many members of Lotta Continua took part; there was also a rally with a speech delivered by Adriano Sofri. *Immediately after this rally, Sofri and Pietrostefani approached me; I remember that we went to have a drink together in a café and then we went off to talk in the street.* They assured me that the decision had been made by the Executive Political Committee, and told me that the time was ripe in part because of the effect produced by the death of Serantini: the decision had already been made, with the same reasoning that had been described to me by Enrico [= Bompressi], but it was tactically useful to move quickly, specifically in order to respond to the death of Serantini, so as to harness the rage that this death had unleashed among the members of the organization. At this point, I expressed my willingness to take part. During this conversation, I was given fairly general instructions: I was told that if we should happen to be arrested, we were to state that we had acted entirely on our own, and wholly on individual initiative, without involving the organization. I was also assured that I would receive legal assistance from lawyers not known to be associated with Lotta Continua, and that I would be given financial assistance should I be injured. I was, however, told nothing about the actual operational plan, except that I should go back to Turin and await further instructions. (*Police Report*, pp. 8–9; emphasis added)

Interrogation of 29 July: Marino, in the presence of Investigating Magistrate Lombardi and Assistant District Attorney Pomarici (thus no longer in the sole presence of Pomarici) confirmed his previous statements. In comparison with the previous version, however, he minimized the presence of Pietrostefani at Pisa: '*I remember perfectly that, following the rally, I withdrew to speak with Sofri and Pietrostefani. On that occasion, I spoke chiefly with Sofri*, who was the recognized leader of LC' (*Preliminary Inquest*, p. 3; emphasis added).

In the interrogation of 17 August, Pietrostefani began to fade around the edges:

I should say that the assassination of Calabresi had already been planned in detail prior to the death of Serantini; if Serantini had not died, Calabresi would have been killed just the same, but the assassination was scheduled about twenty days after the day on which it actually took place. The death of Serantini, in practical terms, served only to hasten the killing. In fact, as soon as we learned of Serantini's death, Pietro [= Pietrostefani] summoned me to Turin and told me that the executive committee had decided to move the date forward, so as to exploit the rage that Serantini's death had triggered among the comrades. Consequently, he added that the killing had already been ordered, and that if I wished to have a confirmation of this and if I wished to speak with Sofri – to whom he knew I was very close – I should go to Pisa, where Sofri would be addressing a rally, and that I could talk to Sofri there, and that Sofri would confirm that this was the decision of the executive committee. That is why I went, with Laura Buffo, to the rally in Pisa, and why I spoke with Sofri, as described previously. *Actually, then, at Pisa I spoke only with Sofri*, because I no longer needed to speak with Pietro, after all our lengthy conversations in Turin concerning the need for the operation and about the plans for it. All I needed was reassurance from Sofri, to the effect that he was in agreement about the operation; only after speaking with him did I give my final commitment to take part in the operation. Also present in Pisa were Brogi and Morini, though they did not witness the conversation between Sofri and myself. *Also present was Pietrostefani, as far as I can*

recall, even though the conversation involved only Sofri and myself.
As I have said, I do not remember Pietrostefani in any way
being involved in the discussion between Sofri and myself,
because I no longer had any reason to speak with him.
(*Preliminary Inquest*, p. 12; emphasis added)

Confrontation (a step in criminal procedure in which witnesses
or accused whose stories disagree are brought face to face to
have it out among themselves, revealing the truth) with Sofri,
16 September 1988:

I wish to state that the decision to kill Police Superintendent Calabresi had already been taken prior to the death of
the anarchist Serantini at Pisa, but the decision was then
made to act immediately in order to respond to that event.
I therefore travelled to Pisa, accompanied by Laura Buffo,
in her car, primarily to speak with Adriano. In Pisa there
were two rallies on that day: one held by the Communist
Party and one held by Lotta Continua. I went to the Lotta
Continua rally, and I took part in it and listened to the
speech delivered by Adriano Sofri. *After the rally, I said hello
to Sofri, and we withdrew to speak, I believe alone,* and on that
occasion Adriano confirmed everything I had been told by
Pietrostefani; he was worried, but he told me that the
decision had been made and he confirmed that it was better
to act sooner than planned. (*Confrontation*, p. 5; emphasis
added)

The lawyer Ascari asked for an explanation of the interjection
'I believe alone'. Marino explained: '*I spoke with him alone* even

though there were a great many people in the square' (*Confrontation*, p. 6; emphasis added).

Sofri and Pietrostefani together; chiefly with Sofri; exclusively with Sofri; with Sofri alone. Over the course of this sequence, the figure of Pietrostefani moves further and further into the distance – but when the investigators ask whether Pietrostefani was physically present among the leaders of Lotta Continua surrounding Sofri after the rally, Marino gives conflicting answers: ('I think that Pietrostefani was present'; 'I do not know whether Pietrostefani was present').[29]

These doubts were not finally resolved until the trial (10 January 1990). The presiding judge forced Marino into a corner. Before our very eyes, Pietrostefani disappears, dissolves: 'I don't remember seeing Pietrostefani . . . I remain personally convinced that he was there, but I cannot, let us say, declare that to be the case for certain. . . . Let me repeat, I spoke only with Sofri at Pisa. Pietrostefani at that moment was not there, I did not see him, and I do not remember him being there' (*Trial*, pp. 72–3).

Moreover, the description of the conversation, is punctuated with other examples of uncertainty and inconsistency. At first, Marino provides a wealth of detail. Interrogation of 17 August:

To complete my description of the episode of the conversation I had with Sofri at Pisa prior to the assassination, while confirming the previous police reports, I should add that Sofri said that he had the greatest confidence in Enrico [= Bompressi] and myself, and he further reassured me, telling me that if, by some chance, I were caught or killed, provision would be made for my family, and especially for my son. My misgivings about the operation were based in part on the fact that I had a young son, and I was worried about him, about what would happen to him if I were killed or arrested. He offered sweeping reassurances, and told me that he would see to everything; in this connection he told me about an industrialist from Reggio Emilia with whom he had already discussed this; if, by chance, I were caught or killed, this industrialist would take care of all of my family's needs. (*Preliminary Inquest*, p. 13)

All this was repeated, point by point, by Marino in the confrontation with Sofri (16 September) with a further notation: 'This conversation lasted about ten minutes' (*Confrontation*, p. 6). Sofri took note, with evident sarcasm. And surely it cannot be easy to cram into such a short time a conversation comprising Marino's dramatic fears, Sofri's explanations and reassurances, and finally Marino's decision to take part in a conspiracy to kill. And yet, in Marino's answers to the presiding judge's queries, those minutes shrink yet further, practically vanishing into thin air: 'This meeting took very little time, I must say . . .' (*Trial*, p. 64); '. . . in practical terms, finally, this conversation did not take up very much time, in the sense that he [Sofri] was fully aware, let us say, of the project, which is to say that I did not waste time discussing practical aspects of it with him' (*Trial*, p. 66). A brief, terse, almost bureaucratic conversation.

Sofri stated that this conversation (which, if proven, would constitute the sole item of incriminating evidence against him) never took place; he added that Marino, while inventing it, forgot two details that make it highly improbable. Sofri pointed them out during the confrontation (*Confrontation*, pp. 6–7). The first item was the heavy rain that was falling on Pisa on the afternoon of 13 May 1972, during and after the rally; the second was the call Marino paid Sofri on the evening of the same day, in the home of Sofri's ex-wife.[30] Why speak on the street in heavy rain, surrounded by policemen, rather than in an apartment where it would have been easy to speak freely, without witnesses?

Further inconsistencies were noted by the presiding judge. In that conversation, Sofri had said 'not to worry, because both he and the other comrades had the greatest confidence in me [*these are Marino's words*] and Ovidio' (*Trial*, pp. 68–9). This, the presiding judge objected, is 'in stark contradiction' with Marino's own previous statement: that for a long time, and still during the period in question, Marino had known and knew Bompressi only as 'Enrico'. Pressed on this matter, Marino retracted what he had just said: Sofri had in fact said 'Enrico'. The same meandering approach characterized Marino's response to questions about the phone call announcing the date of the assassination. Who had told Marino the date? Sofri? Marino had at first denied that it was Sofri, but when he was grilled by the presiding judge, he changed his story – it had been none other than Sofri. 'What?!' exclaimed the judge: 'Just now, just a second ago, you said that it wasn't, Marino. . . . Calm down! A second ago, you said that it wasn't. Now remember, this has all been recorded: so, later, when we play it back. . . . You understand? The impression you are giving is that you say things and then you deny them' (*Trial*, pp. 73–4). A few days later (15 January), the presiding judge, before completing the first session of Marino's trial testimony, raised a new problem. Marino had just admitted that someone called him in Turin, to inform him that everything was set for the assassination: but had he, Marino, informed the others that he was willing to take part? 'In effect,' the presiding judge observed, 'the organizer was still not certain that you would be taking part, and in fact Pietrostefani said to you: "You, Marino, still have some doubts. If you still have doubts, go to Pisa." You went to Pisa and you resolved your doubts. But – and this is the point – did you inform Pietrostefani that you had resolved your doubts?'

Marino: 'No.'
Presiding judge: 'You didn't see Pietrostefani again?'
Marino: 'No.'
Presiding judge: 'Between the 13th and the 17th . . .'
Marino: 'I saw him again . . . no, no . . . I saw him again later . . .'
Presiding judge: 'Nor did you see Enrico [=Bompressi]?'
Marino: 'No.'
Presiding judge: 'Then Enrico had already left on his own?'
Marino: 'Yes, I saw him again in Milan . . .'
Presiding judge: 'What I mean to say is, then, that the go-ahead had been given for the operation, even before you had fully agreed to participate?'
[*Stenographer's note: Marino does not answer the presiding judge's question.*]
Presiding judge: 'Well then, you don't know!'
Marino: 'I don't know.'
Presiding judge: 'The simple fact is that Enrico had already

left prior to the 13th, and then you told Pietrostefani nothing at all about the fact that you were now willing to participate?'

Marino: 'No.' (*Trial*, pp. 281–2)

V I

Luigi Ferrajoli described the trial, as the reader will recall, as 'the only instance of historiographic experimentation'. The judge who questions defendants and witnesses ('sources . . . made to perform *de vivo*') behaves like a historian who compares, and analyses, various documents. But documents (defendants, witnesses) do not speak by themselves. As Lucien Febvre pointed out more than fifty years ago in his inaugural lecture before the Collège de France, to make documents speak we must interrogate them, posing appropriate questions of them:

> . . . a historian does not roam about at random through the past, like a ragman in search of bric-à-brac; rather he sets out with a specific plan in mind, a problem to solve, a working hypothesis to test. If one objects, 'this is not a scientific approach', does one not simply reveal one's fundamental ignorance of science, of its conditions and methods? When a histologist looks through the lens of his microscope, does he immediately grasp the raw facts? The essence of his work consists of creating, as it were, the subjects that he observes, often with the assistance of exceedingly complex techniques; and then, once he has acquired these subjects, 'reading' them, 'reading' his

prepared specimens. A daunting task, in truth. Because to describe what one sees is one thing; but to see that which must be described, that is the hard part.[31]

By now, these considerations sound rather self-evident, at least in principle (in terms of genuine research, they are less than obvious). If we explore the analogy suggested by Ferrajoli, we may try to extend it from the context of history to that of the law. It should come as a surprise to no one that Investigating Magistrate Lombardi and Assistant District Attorney Pomarici were guided, in their preliminary inquest, by 'a specific plan in mind, a problem to solve, a working hypothesis to test'; much less should it come as an outrage. The point is quite different: the quality of the hypotheses developed. These hypotheses must (a) be endowed with considerable explanatory power; and should they be contradicted by the known facts, they must (b) be modified or even abandoned entirely. If this last clause is ignored, the risk of slipping into error (juridical or historical) is unavoidable.

As one reads the transcript of the trial, one has the clear impression that Presiding Judge Minale's initial working hypothesis was quite different from the working hypothesis employed by the Investigating Magistrate Lombardi and Assistant District Attorney Pomarici. During the course of four long sessions of courtroom testimony (9, 10, 11, 12 January 1990), followed by examination and cross-examination by the lawyers (12, 15 January), the presiding judge hammered away at Marino. Gradually, the weak points, inconsistencies, and unlikely details of his confessions emerged. And so serious flaws emerged in the case against those accused of ordering the murder; serious flaws thus emerged in the effort to link Lotta Continua, as an organization, with the assassination of Calabresi. That is not all; Marino's awkward responses to the presiding judge's objections brought to light – as we have seen – a highly improbable circumstance: that the planners of an assassination had not bothered – just four days prior to the planned killing – to make sure that the designated driver (Marino himself) was willing to take part in the operation. As one reads the transcripts of Marino's courtroom testimony, one cannot escape the feeling that the trial was moving, under the guidance of the presiding judge, in a direction quite different from the direction it actually took in the end. Is this an optical illusion, visible only in hindsight? Or was there a shift, a veering away, at a certain point? Could it be that the working hypothesis initially developed by Presiding Judge Minale was modified, in accordance with new elements that emerged during courtroom testimony?

V I I

Let's not even talk about new elements – during the course of testimony, there was a full-fledged show-stopper. On 20 February 1990 a witness called by the court – the *maresciallo*, or sergeant of the *carabinieri*, Emilio Rossi – declared, amid general astonishment, that Marino had first entered the offices of the *carabinieri* of Ameglia on 2 July 1988 – not 19 July, then, as he had said during the preliminary inquest. Sergeant Rossi said that Marino appeared to him 'strange (that is, nervous and a bit tense)'. Marino had said that he wanted to talk about 'sensitive' matters; he began to tell his life story, referring to 'rather grave occurrences' dating back to the time when was a militant in Lotta Continua, twenty years before; and he hinted, without going into detail, at a 'specific event' that seemed to be 'more grave than the others', and had occurred in Milan. Sergeant Rossi got in touch with his immediate superior, Captain Maurizio Meo, commander at Sarzana. Captain Meo met Marino immediately, during the night of 2–3 July. It had been Marino who had asked that the meeting should take place after one in the morning, which was when he finished work (during the summer he sold crêpes from a truck at Bocca di Magra). Once again, Marino had spoken, still without going into detail, of a 'grave occurrence which had taken place in Milan'. On 4 July (3 July was a Sunday), Captain Meo called the group commander, requesting permission to travel to Milan to discuss the case with Lieutenant Colonel Umberto Bonaventura of the Reparto Operativo (Operations Department). On 5 July, Meo met with Bonaventura in Milan; during the night of 5–6 July he met Marino once again in Ameglia; on the night of 7–8 (and then, again, during the night of the 13th and the morning of the 19th) Bonaventura came to Sarzana to meet Marino. All this was confirmed, with the addition of numerous details, by Captain Meo and Lieutenant Colonel Bonaventura, who had also been called on 20 and 21 February to testify before the Milan Court of Assizes (*Trial*, pp. 1582–1635; 1690–1723).

On one crucial point, therefore – the laborious beginning of his confessions – Marino had lied to Investigating Magistrate Lombardi and Assistant District Attorney Pomarici. We now know that the formal inquest they conducted was preceded by a phase, lasting seventeen days, during which Marino had engaged in a series of informal conversations in the *carabinieri* barracks of Ameglia and Sarzana. There are no police reports, no other documentary records of these conversations. And that is not all. They took place at astonishing times, almost always in the middle of the night. The *carabinieri* explain that this was because of Marino's working hours – we learn, however, that he did not work in the morning. And, for that matter, why such consideration for Marino? Here we uncover another oddity, perhaps the oddest of them all: the lack of proportion between Marino's very generic confessions during this phase, and the enormous interest they engender at ever-higher levels of command. Marino's reference to a 'grave occurrence in Milan' some twenty years earlier, followed by the statement that 'he wished to report at higher levels' (this was Sergeant Rossi speaking: *Trial*, pp. 1583–4) had immediate and enormous effect. Captain Meo hastened to meet Marino, even though all he obtained was weeping, declarations of remorse, and the usual reference to a 'grave occurrence which took place in Milan' (*Trial*, p. 1601). Not very much, one might say, but still enough to bring running from Milan, that very same night, no less a figure than Colonel Bonaventura: an expert in the fight against terrorism, and a former right-hand man of General Dalla Chiesa, the *carabinieri* General who took on and defeated left-wing terrorism in Italy in the 1980s, later murdered by the Mafia. Now, Bonaventura had worked repeatedly on the Calabresi murder case. This, however (we are told), was a mere coincidence, because Marino revealed his involvement in the killing of Calabresi only much later, during the preliminary inquest, and specifically on 21 July, during the second interrogation conducted by Assistant District Attorney Pomarici (*Police Report*, pp. 7 ff.).

The first two meetings between Colonel Bonaventura and Marino ended without results. During the course of the third, the colonel spoke more or less as follows (still according to Captain Meo):

> Now, Marino, you have got to make up your mind: really, we can't waste time here talking about your personal problems and the problems of your family, when you certainly came here to tell us something, yet you don't want to tell us this certain something.... Come up to Milan. Let's write something down and see if you make up your mind to tell us something and then something more, so that we can begin to understand what it is that you want to talk about: because it is pointless for you to talk about this grave occurrence ... grave occurrence ... grave occurrence, without ever telling us what it is you want to talk about.

And how did it happen – inquired the presiding judge – that Marino agreed to come to Milan? Captain Meo attempted to answer the question, with a fairly laboured response:

> ... that is, we, at first, had tried to get him to talk and, if possible, to write something or to pressure him on some point and understand what it was he wanted to talk about. There was this clear reluctance on his part to have an open exchange. We made an effort to understand, and perhaps we understood.... 'Maybe it would be better in Milan.... Considering that he committed this grave act in Milan, or

that this act was committed, about which he knows something and wants to tell us ... perhaps Milan can unblock
the situation.' (*Trial*, p. 1615)

'Considering that he committed this grave act in Milan ...' – a
slip of the tongue, quickly covered up ('or that this act was
committed, about which he knows something'). It is clear that
if, in this unrecorded phase of conversation, Marino had confessed to a specific crime, the *carabinieri* would be duty-bound
– once they had performed the appropriate investigations – to
hand Marino over to the appropriate magistrate, so that he
could begin a formal preliminary inquest. Behind this possible
instance of sloppy neglect of proper procedure, however, looms
another, far more unsettling possibility – could it be that during
those seventeen days, in the *carabinieri* barracks in Ameglia and
Sarzana, the assassination of Calabresi was discussed? One
would inevitably come to suspect that Marino's confessions
during the preliminary inquest had been manipulated or even
cooked up in advance, in collaboration with the *carabinieri*.
Colonel Bonaventura's authoritative testimony, however, dis-
pelled all doubt. Everything is plunged into the densest fog,
even the references to Milan that appear periodically in
Marino's testimony:

> The general subject was this: grave occurrences in the
> north of Italy, and so on. Then the reference to Milan ...
> that is: I began to run down, and ... I would say: 'Did
> these occurrences happen in Milan? Did they happen in
> Turin?', and so on ... I became convinced that in effect it
> was something connected with – could be something linked

to – Milan. . . . Why did I develop this belief? Because he told me that he knew Milan, had been to Milan, had spent time in places in Milan. . . . Without clearly making any specific references.

The suspicion that the 'grave occurrence' was the assassination of Calabresi had not dawned upon Colonel Bonaventura until 20 July, in Milan, after the first interrogation, which resulted in a report:

> But when, at a certain point, he said: 'I want to talk to the public prosecutor in Milan and . . . I am terribly afraid; I want to talk to the prosecutor because this is a grave occurrence', at that point it seemed to me that, rather than being simply involved in this grave occurrence, perhaps he was one of the perpetrators of this grave occurrence. So – but that was sort of . . . a kind of intuition on my part. A way of reasoning. It might have been right, it might have been wrong . . . the occurrence was focused on Milan, and there was talk of the year 1972, I think. So, there, no longer generically twenty years ago. And so now the matter was considerably more . . . (21 February 1990; *Trial*, pp. 1705–9)

In the transcript of the interrogation of 20 July, however, the lawyer Gentili (defending Adriano Sofri) pointed out there was no mention of 1972 (*Trial*, p. 1714). Now what?

> Well [explained Colonel Bonaventura], my recollection is that he went on telling us the story of his life, and then he

went on talking about the contacts he had had . . . that he had been in Milan, that he had been in Turin. . . . The fact that I had been able to say that my attention was parallel, that I thought about Calabresi because he said in 1972 – perhaps I was slightly inaccurate, Judge, but in my mind, somehow this subject came up of a grave occurrence in Milan. And so I took him to the public prosecutor, and it couldn't have been anything other than that. Also because he wasn't talking about really old events. Like, say, Piazza Fontana, Annarumma,[32] for instance. His story was not, let us say, rooted in those events. He did not tell me that he had been in Milan, say, in the 1960s. He had not talked about street fighting. . . . So, that is more or less the . . . (*Trial*, pp. 1714–15)

VIII

In the accounts of the three *carabinieri*, everything fits together (almost) perfectly. Their construction, however, is termite-ridden, and at the first hard knock it crumbles into a dust-heap of jumbled phrases. No sensible person would believe that a respected expert on the fight against terrorism would travel three times, in the middle of the night, from Milan to Sarzana, just to listen to vague references to a 'grave occurrence', repeated for hours, punctuated by weeping and long silences, by an unknown crêpe vendor.[33] It is much more persuasive to imagine that Marino, in his meetings with the *carabinieri*, should have spoken of the 'grave occurrence' in much more specific terms, as betrayed by Colonel Bonaventura's slip of the tongue ('the occurrence was focused on Milan, and there was talk of the year 1972'). For that matter, another witness, Captain Meo, trips up in a similar gaffe: '[Marino] identified the grave occurrence as a serious criminal event that took place in Milan and, if I am not mistaken, and in any case it should be written down . . . what is written in the minutes of his testimony, it seems to me that he placed it in 1972, or something of the sort' (*Trial*, pp. 1620–21).

Defence lawyer Gentili pointed out that in the transcripts of the interrogation of 20 July – which took place in the offices of the Nucleo Operativo of the Milan *carabinieri* – there is no mention of 1972. Given that Captain Meo claims to have been present at the interrogation, we can deduce that the transcript is not – on this point, at least – reliable.[34] A disconcerting conclusion. Even more disconcerting, however, was a question from the presiding judge, prompted by the testimony of Captain Meo.

When Colonel Bonaventura heard Marino's name for the first time (Meo recounted), he asked: 'Who is this person?'

'Was the colonel, with the reference to 1972, unable to identify the grave occurrence in question?' inquired the presiding judge (*Trial*, p. 1602).

At the point when the judge uttered these words, neither Captain Meo nor Colonel Bonaventura had yet made any specific reference to the year 1972 in his testimony. To Captain Meo, Marino had spoken of 'events from twenty years ago . . . a grave occurrence that happened in Milan, many years ago' (*Trial*, pp. 1597–8); to Colonel Bonaventura of 'a grave occurrence in Milan . . . some twenty years ago' (*Trial*, p. 1583). The presiding judge's reference would seem entirely unjustified.

One might say that it involuntarily prompted the emergence of
a truth of which the presiding judge himself, Sergeant Rossi,
Captain Meo, Colonel Bonaventura, and of course the defendant, Marino, were all aware: that the account of those unrecorded night-time meetings, set forth in the courtroom with a
great wealth of quaint detail, simply failed to correspond to the
truth. Of course, so grave a supposition could not be based on
a single, unsettling detail.

I X

All the same, in the face of such an array of contradictions and
inconsistencies, how can one be sure that the version of the
facts provided in the courtroom by the three *carabinieri* is the
true version, not simply the last one in chronological order?[35]
Just what Marino and Colonel Bonaventura actually said to
each other in the Sarzana barracks is something that, in all
likelihood, we shall never know. The very existence of those
nocturnal conversations, for that matter, was meant to remain
secret. Fairly unceremoniously, Colonel Bonaventura shifts
responsibility for this forced silence on to the Milanese magistrates: 'We were pretty much constrained . . . by the Judicial
Authority to preserve the strictest secrecy and everything . . .'
(*Trial*, p. 1720).

So – did Lombardi and Pomarici know? Then and there,
Pomarici said that Sergeant Rossi's revelations in the courtroom were complete news to him; then he said, rather, that
the *carabinieri*, after being summoned to testify, had phoned
him to inform him – or perhaps to consult with him – about

what they were going to say in court, and that he, in turn, had advised the chief of the district attorney's office. According to subsequent statements, Pomarici had been aware of Marino's night-time meetings in the *carabinieri* barracks for some time. For how long? And why had he not denounced the false statements that Marino had made, first in the preliminary inquest, and later at the opening of the trial proper?

In his final summation, Pomarici noted that there were those who had wished to find 'something sinister, fishy, dark' in Marino's silence concerning the actual timing of his first informal contacts with the *carabinieri*. If, however, there had been 'something sinister, fishy, dark,' Pomarici objected, the *carabinieri* 'clearly would have covered up for Marino': they would have agreed with him beforehand on a story; therefore 'we would not have seen this straightforward behaviour on the part of the *carabinieri*, who presented themselves in the courtroom to say: no, that is not exactly the way things stand, the first informal contacts began on the 2nd of July, not on 19–20 July. And so I don't understand what sort of conspiracy this would be.'[36] I intend to come back to this conclusion (the non-existence of a conspiracy) later. Concerning the initial premiss, however, we must admit that the *carabinieri*'s straightforward behaviour emerged rather belatedly. Nearly two years had to pass before the official version was denied; and specifically, during the hearing of 20 February 1990, the day on which Sergeant Emilio Rossi broke – presumably in obedience (as we shall see) to orders from above – the seal of silence concerning the seventeen days of talks. Pomarici is right: there was no previously concocted story between Marino and the *carabinieri* on this point, in the sense that the true date was never supposed to have surfaced.

'For twenty months they said nothing about it, and when they did talk about it, it was anything but spontaneously, only because and after they had been summoned to testify in court,' wrote Adriano Sofri, in the memoir he sent to the Milanese judges before they withdrew for deliberations.[37] Why, indeed, were the *carabinieri* summoned to testify?

X

The direct cause can be found in the courtroom testimony given less than a month earlier, on 26 January, by Don Regolo Vincenzi, parish priest of Bocca di Magra. In the preliminary inquest, Marino testified that he had confided in Don Vincenzi, though not in confession, 'immediately prior to the Christmas holidays of 1987' (*Preliminary Inquest*, p. 27); and he had freed him from his bond of secrecy concerning that meeting. Don Vincenzi was summoned to testify (30 July 1988), and he had confirmed this fact. In that context, Marino had told the priest that he had taken part in terrorist acts, and confided that he was deeply remorseful over one very momentous act in particular. Moreover, Marino had told him that he 'was continually being sought out by certain individuals in Bocca di Magra and was even being shadowed; they made dire threats and demanded that he once again engage in criminal acts'; Marino had told these people 'that he had forsaken the world of terrorist crime for ever, and he wanted nothing more to do with it'. In court, Presiding Judge Minale had attempted to learn more about this, but without much success.

Marino, concerning the threats: 'I was not referring to threats at that specific moment. It was a more general matter concerning my life . . . my past life . . . evidently the parish priest sort of misunderstood what I meant to say . . .' (*Trial*, p. 11).

Just who had threatened Marino?

'These were individuals whom I knew from past political experiences. They were people with whom I had once been a political militant. They had taken part in strikes, marches, demonstrations, violent acts, and so on. There was a small circle of people who engaged in illegal acts on behalf of the organization. And so, these individuals were people that I recognized in that setting' (*Trial*, p. 16).

During the course of the trial, however, Marino finally wound up retracting everything he had said: 'When I spoke with the parish priest. . . . When I mentioned threats, I was referring to the threats that I had received years before, and clearly the priest had misunderstood, or else . . .' (*Trial*, p. 51).

Don Vincenzi, too, summoned to testify before the Milan Court of Assizes initially seemed to want to correct, or even to retract, what he had said in the preliminary inquest. He had spoken with Marino at the end of October, not two weeks before Christmas; Marino had appeared relaxed, partly because he had earned reasonable money during the summer. 'And the people who were shadowing him?' the presiding judge asked the priest. Yes, Don Vincenzi remembered that Marino had told him of 'an attempt to drag him into other misdeeds'; there had been no mention, however, of being threatened or followed. The presiding judge appeared surprised, almost menacing ('Look, you are a witness. Sure, of course, having you arrested in court is no longer an option, but . . .'). Don Vincenzi finally confirmed, with evident misgivings, the testimony he had given two years before. Still, the presiding judge would not let up: 'In the days prior to your meeting with Marino, did you see any strangers, any people you did not know, in town?'

Don Vincenzi: 'I saw people in cars in strategic places. I always notice things like that . . . there have been thefts and things before. Not personal attacks; I have my own way of dealing with that. Anyway, I even tried to get them to leave, because they were close to the parish church. One of them showed me a police badge, so I left them alone.'

Presiding judge: 'Yes, this is information we already have. But I meant in town, did you hear Marino talking about people being shadowed, other things . . . ?'

Don Vincenzi: 'I heard people talk about that, certain people, yes. That was after it had happened, however. That they had previously noticed people shadowing day and night, arriving, and leaving. I don't know anything about that myself. I know only about these people in plain clothes who later proved to be from the police.'

Presiding judge: 'No, these other references. . . . These people spoke to you, told you these things, when? After you spoke with Marino?'

Don Vincenzi: 'No, after Marino had been arrested.' (*Trial*, pp. 787–8)

The presiding judge's question about 'strangers', intended to clear up Marino's vague reference (later denied) to being shadowed and threatened by unspecified former terrorist comrades, had an entirely unforeseen effect. Suddenly two different groups of shadowers emerged, one of which (the only one Don Vincenzi encountered directly) consisted of policemen in plain clothes, but carrying badges. When it was the defence's turn to speak, the lawyer Gentili (defending Adriano Sofri) came back to this matter. Don Vincenzi stated specifically that one evening, after he had given testimony (30 July 1988), he had seen a group of young men in a car, and they had driven off before he could take down their licence plate number. (This was probably a group of former members of Lotta Continua, who at the time were conducting a sort of counter-inquest, later published under the title 'Doloroso Mistero', literally 'Woeful Mystery'.) Don Vincenzi's meeting with individuals who had shown a police badge, on the other hand, had taken place 'before Marino was arrested'.

'Before Marino was arrested?' echoed (perhaps in disbelief, or amazement) lawyer Gentili.

Presiding judge: 'Several days before? More or less? But this is an episode . . .'

Don Vincenzi: 'Perhaps a month before. Fifteen days, one month before.'

Lawyer Gentili: 'Do you remember what law enforcement agency they belonged to? That is, were they *carabinieri* or ordinary policemen?'

Don Vincenzi: '*Carabinieri.*' (*Trial*, pp. 791–2)

X I

As the reader will no doubt recall, the version offered by the investigators went like this: Marino, in the throes of remorse, went to the Ameglia *carabinieri* on 19 July 1988, and they took him to Milan; here he began to make his confession and was placed under arrest. The testimony of the three *carabinieri*, intended to replace the now-discredited official version of Marino's confession, was prompted, obviously, by the unexpected revelations of Don Vincenzi.[38] This connection is passed over in silence in the retrospective memoir written by the presiding judge prior to the end of the trial: '. . . this circumstance emerged because the court insisted on hearing the testimony of the sergeant and the captain – otherwise, we would have withdrawn for deliberations with the date of the 19th' (*Trial*, p. 2155). And that is not all. On three different occasions, the presiding judge was confronted with the information that Marino, two weeks or a month before his arrest, was already being shadowed or followed by the *carabinieri*, and every time the presiding judge tried to change the subject: 'Yes, this is the information we already have . . .'; 'No, this other information . . .'; 'But this is an episode . . .'.

'. . . information we already have . . .' – to tell the truth, at that point this information was not known, officially, at all. We have seen, however, that Pomarici was, by his own admission, aware of the actual date of the first contacts between Marino and the *carabinieri* – even though at first Pomarici had said quite the opposite. What about Presiding Judge Minale? To think that he learned of this fact shortly thereafter, in courtroom testimony, directly from Sergeant Emilio Rossi, seems rather improbable. The rapid exchange that began the hearing of 20 February (Presiding judge: 'Did Marino ever come to you, to ask you to help him, or to have you put him in touch with anyone else?' Rossi: 'Yes.' Presiding judge: 'When did he come?' Rossi: 'He came to see me precisely on 2 July 1988.' Presiding judge: 'And so not on 20 July ... not on 19 July.' Rossi: 'On 2 July 1988 ...') has every appearance of being intended for an unsuspecting public. As we read the transcripts of the hearing with the benefit of hindsight, we get the impression that the timing (and the details) of Marino's 'confession' were shrouded, from the very beginning of the trial, in a mist of embarrassment. The first hearing (9 January 1990), after the lawyers' usual procedural skirmishing, began as follows:

Presiding judge: 'You [Marino] have been questioned first by the *carabinieri* and then by the prosecuting attorney and finally by the investigating magistrate, repeatedly. You also took part in several confrontations. Do you confirm what you said? Do you have anything to add or change in what you said before we begin?'

Marino: 'I confirm the manner and timing of the interrogations, and I confirm everything that I stated during those interrogations.'

[*The question was a mere formality; Marino did not realize that, and said too much.*]

Presiding judge: 'What do you mean by the manner and timing of the interrogations? ... Does that mean anything in particular?'

Marino: 'Well, it seemed to me that there are people who have something to say about my interrogations ...'

Presiding judge: 'That is irrelevant. The interrogations were conducted . . . on the dates of the police reports, and so you can do no more than to confirm that.' (*Trial*, p. 7)

Then, and there, it might seem like an obvious thing to say. It becomes a little less so when we think of Marino's night-time meetings, neither recorded nor transcribed, in the *carabinieri* barracks at Ameglia and Sarzana. That is what Presiding Judge Minale must have thought in retrospect, when he reconsidered this give and take towards the end of the trial, reading over and commenting upon it in the courtroom. After recalling his own surprise at the phrase used by Marino ('manner and timing of the interrogations'), the presiding judge commented: 'And I, being unaware of this matter of the month . . .' (*Trial*, p. 2174). We have every reason to doubt that he had been unaware. The reason is quite simple.

A chronology of Marino's so-called confession which differed substantially from the official chronology had already been supplied – perhaps involuntarily – by *carabinieri* Colonel Lorenzo Nobili on 28 July 1988, at the press conference held immediately after the arrest of the (alleged) perpetrators of the assassination of Luigi Calabresi. During this press conference (as we learn from the transcript of the tape recording that Presiding Judge Minale ordered played in the courtroom) Marino, unnamed, is described as follows:

From 1969 on, he was a member of Lotta Continua. After years of inner struggle and long reflection, he declared to the officers of the judiciary police of the Nucleo Operativo of the *carabinieri* of Milan that he wished to free his conscience of a heavy burden that he had been carrying within him for years.

'And this was when?' asked an unidentified journalist.

'Two months ago,' replied an unidentified voice.

Nobili: 'I can't tell you that; this is something that the investigating magistrate would know.'

'Colonel, you should know that: two months? A month?' insisted another journalist.

Nobili: 'Yes, a few months ago. A few months ago. A few months ago.' (*Trial*, p. 2130)

This phrase, pronounced as it was on 28 July, implied a date that not only considerably preceded the date that was proffered shortly thereafter by the investigators (19 July), but also preceded the date that emerged later during the trial (2 July). Was this a mistake on the part of Colonel Nobili, forced into the unfamiliar role of describing the results of a preliminary inquest conducted by others – in this case, the magistrates Lombardi and Pomarici? The idea of a mistake seems rather unlikely. Let us listen to Nobili as he describes the process whereby Marino repented and decided to confess: 'He is a young man who has experienced moments of moral desolation such that, I believe, he confided in a priest, confessed his sins, and then . . . contacted a representative of the *carabinieri*, with whom he began this conversation, very drawn out, very rigorous, extending over a lengthy period of time . . .' (*Trial*, pp. 2133–4).

'. . . extending over a lengthy period of time . . .' – an expression that can hardly be used to describe a dialogue lasting a single day (the investigator's version); and perhaps inappropriate even for an exchange extending from 2 to 20 July (Rossi–Meo–Bonaventura's version). Naturally, Colonel Nobili's words may be tainted by the emphatically triumphant notes of an announcement of a victory. Still, we must wonder, how long had the *carabinieri* been interested in Marino?

XII

We do not know. We do know, however, that throughout most of the trial, Marino told a series of wild lies about his confession. At the preliminary inquest, he said that he had spoken to the *carabinieri* sergeant in Ameglìa. On 12 January, lawyer Pecorella (one of the lawyers defending Bompressi) asked: 'Now, the sergeant in Ameglia with whom you spoke – had you ever met him before? Had you ever had reason to contact him before? And especially if it is not recorded, can you tell us what his name is?'

Presiding judge: 'To him, he was just the sergeant in Ameglia.'

[We should point out here that the trial was being conducted in accordance with the old Italian judicial code: the presiding judge acts as a filter between lawyers and defendants, or between lawyers and witnesses. Here, however, the presiding judge does more than restate the question put to Marino – he actually speaks in Marino's place. The exchange that ensues clearly shows that this is something more than a chance distraction.]

Pecorella: 'Yes, it may be that he met him. . . . Ameglia is not very big, so . . .'

Presiding judge: 'Answer!'

Marino: 'I first knew the sergeant in Ameglia as . . . I had seen him occasionally, but not. . . . My relations with him. . . . That is to say, there was absolutely no relationship. In the sense that the only relations were of the sort. . . . If there was a fine to be paid, I would go in and pay it.[39] But not . . .'

Pecorella: 'Did you know his last name?'

Marino: 'No. I learned that later. . . . His name is Rossi.'

Pecorella: 'Do you know . . . whether by chance he telephoned, or in any other way . . . whether for your trip to Milan he also contacted the *carabinieri* of La Spezia? Or were you taken immediately to Milan?'

Marino: 'Are you asking me that?'

Pecorella: 'Yes, if you know. If you heard the phone call . . .?'

Marino: 'No, I don't know.'

Pecorella: 'But you will surely know this. That is, where did you sleep the night of 20 to 21 July?'

Presiding judge: 'We have already asked him these things. You went to the sergeant and the sergeant directed you to contact the captain of Sarzana. You said: "I want to speak", and you were taken to Milan.'

Marino: 'I don't really understand the question.'

Presiding judge: 'When you were in Sarzana and you said to the captain: "I want to tell you about an event that happened in Milan. I want to speak with the public prosecutor in Milan" – what time was it? Afternoon . . . evening . . .?'

Marino: 'It was evening.'

Presiding judge: 'Then, did they take you immediately to

Milan, or did you sleep there in the barracks ...? Did you go home?'

Marino: 'No, no. He sent me back home.'

Presiding judge: 'And then what happened?'

Marino: 'We made an appointment for the next day. He told me to come back, and then they took me to Milan.'

Presiding judge: 'The next day in Sarzana?'

Marino: 'Yes.'

Pecorella: 'Which was the 20th. On the 20th they came to Milan. I asked between the 20th and the 21st in Milan.'

Presiding judge: 'The 20th and the 21st. Once you were in Milan? You got to Milan, you went to the *carabinieri* of Milan. You were questioned. Then, when the questioning was over, where did you sleep? In the evening, once you had reached Milan? It is 5 p.m. .... At night, between the 20th and the 21st, once you had been questioned by the *carabinieri*, before you were questioned by the prosecuting attorney. Did you sleep? Where did you stay? Marino. ... In any case, we can ask the people who made the report. ... It is not a problem. ...'

Marino: 'I went back ... went back home. Now I don't remember exactly.'

Presiding judge: 'You went back home, and then the morning after? Did you come back to Milan?'

Marino: 'When I. ... Yes, evidently, yes.'

Presiding judge: 'Then, did you come back to Milan on your own?'

Marino: 'When?'

Presiding judge: 'The next day. When you were questioned by the prosecuting attorney.'

Marino: 'No, I was always accompanied by the *carabinieri*. Even when I came up on the 25th. They always took me.'

Presiding judge: 'And so, on the evening of the 20th, the *carabinieri* took you back home, and then they brought you back in the morning?'

Marino: 'Yes. I think so. Now. . . . Because of all the times that I went back and forth, it was always the *carabinieri* who took me.'

Presiding judge: 'So, even after the 21st, you would go back home and then you would come back to Milan?'

Marino: 'Yes, I went back and forth two or three times. Now exactly . . . I don't remember exactly which days.' (*Trial*, pp. 227–9)

Marino doesn't know, he can't remember, he becomes confused even when he is answering such apparently innocuous questions as the one about the *carabinieri* sergeant in Ameglia (whom Marino, apparently, actually knew quite well[40]). The presiding judge seems to be trying to lead Marino in his answers, and in one case Marino follows on his heels, visibly bewildered ('I don't really understand the question'). With the benefit of hindsight, it is easy to sense the subterranean tensions ruffling the surface of the dialogue. The question raised by lawyer Pecorella grazed a hollow spot, which was meant to remain shrouded in secrecy – the unrecorded conversations between Marino and the *carabinieri*. Marino became irritated; when Pecorella asked another question, Marino had an outburst ('Let's not talk nonsense!'). Immediately thereafter, he asked for a recess. The stenographer 'notes that during this entire last part of Marino's testimony, in listening to the tape, one can hear a partial alteration in his voice (stammering, brief interruptions, and so on) and a continual drumming of the fingers' (p. 235). When the court reconvened, Marino said he had a headache. Testimony was suspended. It was Friday, and the hearing was adjourned until the following Monday.

XIII

Even a reading of the transcripts clearly reveals that Marino was a punch-drunk boxer at the end of the hearing of 12 January; that he was saved from complete collapse only by the bell. This situation was probably unexpected; added to it, two weeks later, was the equally unexpected testimony of Don Regolo Vincenzi. In the face of extreme difficulties, extreme measures are in order. Better to sacrifice the preliminary inquest than lose the whole trial. And without a doubt the testimony, in a hierarchic crescendo, of the three *carabinieri* would seem to have delivered a fatal blow to the preliminary inquest – fatal, at least, at first glance. Upon closer inspection, however, we see that their testimony achieved the opposite effect. Re-establishing the truth, with the air of those who do exactly as they please – with disregard even for Investigating Magistrate Lombardi and Assistant District Attorney Pomarici – the *carabinieri* actually buttressed the conclusions of both Lombardi and Pomarici; by pointing out Marino's deceitfulness on a specific point (however important) they reiterated the overall truthfulness of his confessions. All we need to do is examine how, with varying emphasis, the three *carabinieri* proposed once again, to the court of Milan and to public opinion at large, the central theme of the preliminary inquest – Marino's repentance and confession – which Presiding Judge Minale had initially helped to dismantle.[41]

Sergeant Emilio Rossi had noted Marino's disturbed state:

> ... in this short account that he gave, I noticed that, for instance, he would turn and look around as if there were someone staring at him: in brief, he was not calm; that is, he was agitated, and I could see that he was sweating and he would smoke ... I saw that he was unquestionably worried; that is, you can see if a person is ... from the way they move; that is, a person who sweats as they speak and who looks around wildly.... That is, I could see that, in effect, there were some problems.... (*Trial*, p. 1583)

Captain Maurizio Meo had detected, alongside the personal turmoil, remorse:

> He would say to me: 'You may be amazed that I come to you and tell you now about things that happened twenty years ago; and after all I am now leading a normal life, a tranquil life; I have a wife and children, I have my work, and you could say that I am settled here.... However, you understand, I have to deal with my conscience as well, I have to look my children in the eyes and, even if this will hurt them, I have to speak and I have to be able to look my children in the eyes', and this was a recurring theme with him. Moreover, he was very upset, because he was very nervous, he waved his hands a great deal and would chain-smoke. I can't recall if he had cold sweats ... [*Stenographer's note: difficult to understand*] (in the sense that drops

of sweat would fall) or whether he would weep – in any case, he had problems, and was, in short, clearly upset and confused. (Captain Maurizio Meo, *Trial*, p. 1599; see also pp. 1607, 1609)

Colonel Umberto Bonaventura also insisted on the theme of remorse, in more elusive terms:

> ... And at the end [of the first conversation] I can't say that I was very well satisfied, because I can't say that I had achieved very much. The occurrence, he says, yes ... I am terribly remorseful, and now this and now that. No, absolutely not. However, well, I thought to myself that, in short, I should be patient and maybe. ... And the second time I found him ... he even greeted me with a smile. Now, let me make an effort to remember. He greeted me with a smile, and so I said: 'Well then, it looks like you are calmer, you trust me. We can talk, we can go. ...' And he said to me: 'Yes, because, you know. ...' And he starts up again talking about his children, his children were very important to him; he went on about how it was important to turn himself in now that they were grown up because ... and he began to go into detail, let us say, talking to me about the activities of Lotta Continua, of an occupation ... the occurrence. ... Now, more specifically, let us say the fact that he had taken part in a demonstration inside the Fiat plant, which was a landmark to all the Fiat factory workers at that time; that he had given ... his children had been born, and he had named them after Adriano Sofri and Pietrostefani. (*Trial*, pp. 1695, 1697)[42]

'He began to go into detail' ... 'Now, more specifically, let us say' ... after which, as respected an expert in the field of terrorism as Bonaventura serves up to the court a series of generic statements, tautologies and errors. Be that as it may. What was important was to reinforce the keystone of the preliminary inquest: the genuine quality of Marino's repentance, and therefore of his confessions, which Investigating Magistrate Antonio Lombardi had described – as the reader will recall – as 'the leading source of proof in this trial'.

XIV

Judge Lombardi did not say (though he probably knew) that this trial was based to a very large extent on the confessions of a self-confessed defendant/witness who, over the course of seventeen days at least, had engaged in informal (and therefore unrecorded) night-time conversations with the *carabinieri*. We have seen that those conversations had been meant to remain secret, at least as far as the judicial authorities were concerned. The belated honesty of Sergeant Rossi and his superiors, so highly praised by Pomarici, was not enough to eliminate a lingering doubt that their disclosures had been offered in order to put the trial back on track after it was unexpectedly derailed. The question that Presiding Judge Minale put to Marino before the end of the trial – why had he lied about the beginning of his contacts with the *carabinieri*? (*Trial*, pp. 2155–6) – really ought to have been put to the *carabinieri* and the investigating magistrates. What had there been to hide in the extensive meetings (how long they went on, we do not know) between Marino and the *carabinieri* officers? This question immediately prompts another: are we looking at an adulterated trial, a conspiracy?

During the course of the trial, two Milanese newspapers (*Il Giornale* and *Il Corriere della Sera*) wondered in print – for reasons that we shall soon examine – whether there might not be a Communist plot underlying the investigation of Sofri and his fellow defendants. In a declaration given to the newspapers on 27 January 1990, Sofri rejected as 'ridiculous the idea of a plot on the part of the Italian Communist Party, the *carabinieri*, or anyone else', adding:

> I have not spoken of, nor imagined, a Communist plot, for two reasons: the first a matter of method, since seeing conspiracies is an easy and ruinously paranoid approach; the second is a matter of fact, because I am convinced that the original recipe of the dish that I have been served is decidedly a piece of home cooking, and specifically from the kitchen of Signor and Signora Marino.[43]

Two very clear statements, which we should discuss separately.

I shall begin with the question of method.[44] Here I seem to detect a note of self-criticism. The reliance upon the initiative of the masses theorized by Lotta Continua implied a continual polemic against the short cuts of terrorism – but it did not by any means rule out, especially between the late sixties and early seventies, a tendency to attribute conspiracies, real or imagined, to sectors of the establishment and state. When I say 'real or imagined', I am already referring to the root of my disagreement with Sofri, one of the many disagreements that have served to nourish our friendship right up to the time of writing (though in this case, the disagreement has more to do with the form than the substance). In Italy, the term 'conspiracy' has been used for about a decade, primarily in a pejorative context: almost inevitably, it has been used in order to state that there are no conspiracies, or that conspiracies exist only in the feverish imaginations of *dietrologi* (a term coined more recently, and with even more distinctly pejorative connotations). Now, there can be little or no doubt that what has been written about conspiracies and *dietrologie*,[45] always and everywhere, amounts to a vast library of foolishness, often with ruinous consequences. Yet one cannot deny that conspiracies do exist. In modern states, special institutions (intelligence agencies) have been established to create and uncover them. Of course, it is considered appropriate, among those who do not wish to be thought naive, to speak of intelligence agencies in tones of derisive superiority: an attitude that seems truly odd, considering that we live in a world that was ruled until recently by two superpowers governed, respectively, by the former director of the CIA and the protégé of the late head of the KGB.

Historians of the contemporary era might do well to wonder whether this coincidence is an indication of a new phenomenon: a specific, relatively autonomous role played to a growing extent by the intelligence agencies on the international scene. It seems unlikely that this hypothesis can be applied to Italy. The murky and bloody game of mass slaughter, misinformation, *dossiers* and extortion that has been under way in Italy for the past twenty years or more seems to have been firmly governed by political forces making use of the secret services (and the factions that struggle within them), not the other way round.

Any historian, however, who attempted to decipher this affair while renouncing, a priori, any *dietrologico* attitudes would not get far – if by *dietrologia* we mean a clear-eyed interpretative scepticism, unwilling to settle for the surface explanations of events or texts. For instance, to read the transcripts of the interrogations of Aldo Moro by the Red Brigades without wondering about the circumstances of their discovery, in the so-called 'lair' in the Via Montenevoso, by the *carabinieri* commanded by General Dalla Chiesa, then immediately joined by Assistant District Attorney Ferdinando Pomarici (well, look who it is again!), would be an act of naiveté.[46] This is not an example taken at random: in part because it seems relevant to me (an observation that some will see as *dietrologica*) that the *dietrologia*, in a largely ironical context, entered the language shortly after the kidnap and murder of Aldo Moro, an event surrounded by multiple layers of conspiracies – real and false. I emphasize the use of the plural – 'conspiracies' – which helps to ward off the risk of simplification that underlies the use of this notion. A conspiracy always tends to engender other conspiracies: real conspiracies that tend to take control of it, fictitious conspiracies that tend to hide it, conspiracies of opposing allegiance that tend to counter it.[47] Far more important, however, is the fact that every action directed towards an objective – and therefore, *a fortiori*, every conspiracy, which is an action directed towards particularly chancy objectives – enters into a system of unpredictable and heterogeneous forces. On the interior of this complex network of actions and reactions, which involve social processes that cannot easily be manipulated, the heterogeneity of objectives with respect to the initial intentions is the rule. Anyone who fails to take this fundamental consideration into account tends to mix intentions with facts and proclamations (at times grotesquely disproportionate) with events, slipping into extreme forms of judicial historiography.[48]

Now let us move on to the second reason – not of method but of fact – mentioned by Sofri in his memoir: that the entire affair sprang from the lies of Leonardo Marino and his wife, the astrologer Antonia Bistolfi. It seems to me that this rather hasty statement served, at the time, chiefly to discourage efforts to exploit the trial for largely political (anti-Communist) reasons. The defence memoir delivered by Sofri to the judges in Milan, drawn up at the end of the hearing, suggested a more complex hypothesis, insisting on the different forms taken on over time by the doings of the couple Marino–Bistolfi.[49] Let us now attempt to present them in chronological order, prefacing them with a rapid reference to an episode that may not be entirely extraneous to the case. In 1980, Leonardo Marino and Antonia Bistolfi formed a friendship with a married couple, Luisa Castiglioni and Hans Deichmann, who, three years later, gave them lodging in their villa at Bocca di Magra. Later still, the relationship turned sour; Marino (who, together with his wife, had agreed to work as custodian and gardener of the villa) had attempted to sue Deichmann for labour law violations. It just so happens that Deichmann's son, Mathias, formerly a militant in a far-left group, was mentioned in an article in the weekly magazine *Epoca* in 1972 as the killer of Calabresi; the article contained details (such as a first, unsuccessful attempt by the killers) that were later presented as top secret. A truly odd coincidence, which aroused absolutely no interest in Presiding Judge Minale. Hans Deichmann's courtroom testimony was hurried along in a thoroughly bureaucratic manner (*Trial*, pp. 1891–6). The possibility that Deichmann might have spoken to Marino about an episode that had burdened him grievously for a number of years was scarcely touched upon.

Let us, however, move on to the doings of the couple Marino–Bistolfi.

1. At the beginning of summer 1987, Antonia Bistolfi, at the invitation of the Sarzana commissioner of culture, delivered a lecture on astrology in the town hall. She stated that on that occasion she met Ovidio Bompressi, who was looking for graphic artists to work on a new magazine about Sarzana. (In reality, as Bompressi's defence lawyer pointed out, the dates don't tally; only two issues of the magazine, *Costa Ovest*, were published, in summer 1986 [*Trial*, pp. 889–90].) At that point, Bistolfi recalled an observation confided to her fifteen years before by a friend, Laura Vigliardi Paravia, at the time a houseguest of Bistolfi in Turin. Bistolfi then paid a call on a lawyer in La Spezia, Zolezzi, telling him that she was in fear of her life: she informed him 'that ... Laura Vigliardi Paravia [had told her] that the man who had shot Calabresi was this gentleman, whom I had always called Enrico, and whom I knew perfectly well was actually named Ovidio Bompressi, and then I really didn't know at all ...' (29 January 1990; *Trial*, p. 825). During the course of the same deposition, Bistolfi added further details concerning that day fifteen years before: she had been in the kitchen with Laura, while Bompressi was in another room:

> and she [Laura] was very ... well, how should I put it? ... agitated, and I couldn't think of another word to

describe it, and – well, she said to me: 'Hey. . . . It's him!',
and I didn't even understand what she was talking about.
I didn't understand, and she tossed this newspaper on to
the table, just like that, folded, and there was an Identikit,
which until that very moment had made no particular
impression on me, you see, and I hadn't even. . . . She said
to me: 'Don't you see, it's his spitting image?', and I looked
at it, and the only thing I noticed . . . that his hair was just
a little lighter in colour; however, this remained in a sort
of limbo, all of this and that, because it seemed like such
an unearthly odd thing, that I said: 'Huh . . .' and that conversation ended right there, and was never mentioned again
in any way or any form. (29 January 1990; *Trial*, p. 831)

We shall soon see the origins and implications – truly astonishing – of this reference to the 'hair . . . just a little lighter in
colour'. Here, the important thing is to note that despite the
objections of the presiding judge, Bistolfi was unable to discern
any difference whatsoever between this account and what,
according to the preceding version, she had told lawyer Zolezzi
('the man who had shot Calabresi', and so on). And why had
she decided to call on the lawyer? After all, she had met Bompressi frequently, even recently. When the presiding judge
asked her to explain clearly the 'specific feeling' which, according to Bistolfi, had prompted her to go and see the lawyer, she
responded:

Yes, this incredible feeling of disquiet came: *first*, from
the feeling that there was no way to make a living and I
didn't know how I was going to support my family; this

gentleman popped out of another ... in my head, from another context, not the town hall or a magazine or the graphic artists; I didn't know about this and I never even knew what his job was; and there he was, in the town hall, and then he goes upstairs and downstairs, and so on; in any case, in general, I said this during the preliminary inquest: I told this to Judge Lombardi, because he was trying to understand it too. . . . I told him: 'I went to lawyer Zolezzi, because I did not feel that I was among friends', and that is what best describes the state of mind I was in, you see, and I felt that I was trapped in a disturbing situation; and, since my nerves were absolutely shot from not knowing how I was going to feed my children, and since, obviously, underlying all this affair was the secret that Laura Buffo had told me, and which I had blotted out, and put who-knows-where, at home, in my pocket, you see . . . (*Trial*, p. 821)

Summoned to testify (25 January 1990), lawyer Zolezzi confirmed only part of this jumble of nonsense. Bistolfi had spoken to him only about a secret confided to her long before, in Turin, by a woman who had information about a particularly grave occurrence. She had seemed confused and upset (Zolezzi regretted not having taken her seriously); in any case, she had never mentioned Calabresi (*Trial*, pp. 760 ff.).

2. Between the end of September and the beginning of October 1987 (the date was subsequently corrected to 'the end of October'; during the preliminary inquest, he had said 'on a day prior to the Christmas holidays'), the parish priest of Bocca

di Magra, Don Regolo Vincenzi, was approached by Marino. As we have already noted, Marino told the priest that he had been involved in 'exceedingly grave occurrences and criminal acts', including terrorist acts; he had also referred to 'the spilling of blood', including one 'particularly serious' episode (26 January 1990; *Trial*, pp. 772 ff.), without, however, mentioning names.

3. Roughly two months before turning himself in (therefore, around May 1988) Marino spoke to a politician from his own party: the Communist former senator Flavio Bertone, deputy mayor of Sarzana. In court, Marino spoke at first, vaguely, of speaking to a 'public figure' about the 'political' aspects of the murder; later, Bertone's name emerged. On 26 January 1990 Bertone appeared to testify, reluctant and reticent. He could not remember the exact date of his meeting with Marino (he does not own a desk diary); no one recommended that he speak to Marino (he receives visitors without appointments). He said that Marino had confided in him that he had taken part in the assassination of Calabresi 'on orders that had been given *to him* by the clandestine group within Lotta Continua, and specifically by Sofri'; that Marino had spoken of Sofri 'bitterly'; that he had also mentioned the name of Pietrostefani (a detail that Bertone had forgotten then and there), but certainly not the name of Bompressi. Bertone said that at the end of their talk, he had urged Marino to reflect: if he continued to remain in this 'bitter, tortured state of mind', it would be best to turn to the police or a magistrate (26 January 1990; *Trial*, p. 796). A few days later Bertone contacted a lawyer, who advised him to mention his meeting with Marino to nobody. He stated that he

said nothing even to lawyer Zolezzi, whom he described as a close friend. In response to a question from lawyer Gentili, he denied ever having advised Marino to hire as a defender another lawyer to whom he was close, Maris (a Communist); Marino had in fact hired Maris. At this point, a commotion erupted in court, and Sofri interjected with a brusque question of Maris – was it not true that Maris had called Bertone to find out whether he would take part in the preliminary inquest? Maris became indignant, but he made no denial. On the next day (27 January), Sofri rejected – as noted above – the rumours of a 'Communist conspiracy'.

And rightly so, because the idea of a 'Communist conspiracy' is a crude and simplistic one. None the less, the hypothesis – expressed at first by Sofri – that the entire affair was the product of a lie crafted by the couple Leonardo Marino and Antonia Bistolfi is just as improbable. The series of events that we have set forth here cannot be easily pigeonholed. Is this a construction that gradually emerged? Or an array of disconnected fragments? Or a progression of ever larger Chinese boxes? Only this last hypothesis would be compatible with the idea of a conspiracy.

A conspiracy, however, is, by definition, difficult to prove. One might make use of indirect evidence. Could the repeated disappearance of evidence itself be considered evidence? The clothing that Calabresi was wearing on the day he was murdered disappeared in 1972, and no one was ever able to examine it. The dark-blue Fiat 125 used by the killers, as noted in a memo from police inspector Francesco Pedullà, was 'demolished on 31 December 1988' – five months after the accused were arrested – 'having been parked in the Fiorenza car lot since 25 August 1972'. The bullet that killed Calabresi was actually auctioned off, following flood damage to the criminal evidence office.[50] Strange coincidences. But these are exactly the sort of things that happen frequently in Italy – suffice it to mention the disappearance, during the course of the preliminary inquest, of the price tags from the suitcases that held the explosive used in the murderous bombing of Piazza Fontana (Milan, 1969).

Let us return to Marino and his confessions. What we have seen taking shape is an exquisitely Italian itinerary, beginning with a lawyer of the Republican Party, Zolezzi, continuing with a priest (Don Regolo Vincenzi) and a Communist deputy mayor (Bertone), and concluding at last, after a year, in a *carabinieri* barracks. In the face of this twisting, winding path, it is difficult to accept the hypothesis that the accusations set forth by Marino were the product of a deeply felt, dolorous moral conversion.[51]

X V

And this, rather, as the reader will recall, was the explanation offered by Marino to the investigating magistrates, and accepted without question: 'For many years, the persuasion had been taking root within me, dictated by moral and religious feelings, that I should confess to the appropriate authorities concerning acts and circumstances in which I had been involved. ... Even though I may feel that many may look upon this statement with scepticism, I have decided to confess those things that I have done and those about which I have knowledge. . . .'

Anyone who is accustomed by profession to read and interpret texts can hardly fail to think that these phrases reek of pretentious diction. We should not forget, however, that they have been sifted through a filter of stilted bureaucratic language. Marino must have spoken in a different manner. Impressions, after all, count for little in such a weighty context – or perhaps we should say that they count only if they are based on concrete facts. The problem is that these same phrases are troubling in terms of content as well. Marino has supplied inconsistent accounts of the remarkably slow process of his inner struggle: in the first interrogation during the preliminary inquest (20 July 1988) he narrowed down his reference to 'many years', specifying 'three to four years'; the following day, on the other hand, he stated that he had 'begun to experience a deep-seated crisis of conscience, to the point that he began to withdraw, limiting himself to an entirely legal militancy' immediately after the murder of Calabresi (*Police Report*, p. 16). When did this crisis begin – in 1972 or in 1984–85? In any case, even after the crisis had begun – whenever that may have been – Marino took part in numerous armed robberies (the last of them during the first few months of 1987 [*Police Report*, p. 29]), as well as in a mass assault on the Turin headquarters of the labour organization CISNAL, undertaken 'in the summer of 1974, or at any rate during a summer month' (*Police Report*, p. 28) – in the end, it proved to have been in January.[52]

At the beginning of the trial, as the reader will recall, Presiding Judge Minale seemed to harbour considerable doubt about the authenticity of Marino's repentance, if not about the overall foundation of the preliminary inquest. We have wondered what facts led him to develop such a radically differing opinion, shared by the other judges of the court. We may rule out the idea that he was so persuaded by the revelations offered by the *carabinieri* during the hearings of the 20th and 21st of February – if for no other reason than that the presiding judge had already been aware of these new developments. Let us discard without further ado the hypothesis – which would take us back to the idea of a conspiracy – of a change of direction due to external pressures: a supposition that would be defamatory if it were applied to a magistrate, and which we do not wish to take into consideration for even an instant. All that is left us is to acknowledge what did in fact happen over the course of the hearings: Presiding Judge Manlio Minale, after raising serious and troubling objections to the testimony of the defendant Marino, ended up accepting the veracity of Marino's confessions. That Minale at a certain point seems to have opted for a new working hypothesis – pretty much in line with the working hypothesis that governed the preliminary inquest – is evident, beginning at least with the questioning of the eyewitnesses to the killing of Calabresi, which began during the hearing of 31 January. From the witnesses' testimony emerged a series of elements (I analyse a number of them below) that fail to square with Marino's confessions. The attitude of the presiding judge leads us to think that he must have followed the remarkable methodological criterion set forth by Judge Lombardi: where there is a divergence between the eyewitnesses and Marino, Marino's confessions must be preferred as being closer to the truth.

(a) *The accident in the parking lot.* In court (10 January 1990; p. 103) Marino said, substantially confirming the version he had given during the preliminary inquest (*Police Report*, p. 12):

> As I was driving out of the parking lot, I had in fact this small collision [*a fender-bender – Author's note*] with another car which, evidently, was looking for a parking place (was driving into the parking lot). The accident scared me a bit, because I was driving a stolen car, and I certainly could not show this gentleman the registration of the automobile or stop to argue, and so, with a glance, I indicated to him ... (I made a gesture with one hand, for this gentleman to reverse slightly, so as to clear the way, as it were, and indicating to him that I would stop immediately afterwards to give him my documents or whatever). This gentleman reversed for a short distance, and I, in fact, as soon as the way was clear, took off suddenly, towards the exit of the parking lot (in practical terms, the road away from the parking lot).

In the earliest leaks concerning the preliminary inquest, published in the press in summer 1988, Marino's account of this accident was given as evidence of the authenticity of his confessions. Only someone who had taken part in the assassination would have been able to describe correctly an event which, sixteen years earlier, had been reported inaccurately in the press as having occurred after the killing rather than before. At the preliminary inquest Marino said that he had talked with Pietrostefani about this inaccuracy at the time, and that he had attributed it to an effort to disseminate misinformation on the part of the police. Actually, as lawyer Dinoia pointed out during the course of the hearing (15 January 1990; *Trial*, pp. 285–6), the accident had been reported correctly by *La Stampa* and two other newspapers, which also published small charts showing the dynamics of the collision. Again, Dinoia pointed out that Giuseppe Musicco (the person driving the other car, a Simca 1000, which Marino supposedly hit) gave a radically different account of the accident, an account he confirmed during the hearing (31 January 1990; *Trial*, pp. 921 ff.).

'I was parked', he had said, 'in my car near the subway entrance; but then, as I was driving out of the parking lot, at the intersection a car went by at high speed; it smashed into me and knocked me around and I didn't see a thing; I stopped and didn't see another thing' – he saw nothing of the assassination, which took place a few minutes later. He was driving out of the lot, not into it: 'I was parked *in* the lot, you see, and I was about to drive away,' Musicco insisted, after further questioning, before an on-site inspection – the only one of the entire trial – ordered by Presiding Judge Minale (28 February 1990; *Trial*, p. 1962). As for the silent dialogue with the other driver, Musicco's version, as we have seen, rules that out entirely.

(*b*) *The timing*. Here are Marino's activities prior to the assassination, according to his account, as given during the preliminary inquest (*Preliminary Inquest*, pp. 12–13), later modified here and there during the trial (10 January 1990; *Trial*, pp. 101 ff.; 15 January 1990; *Trial*, pp. 282 ff.). Around 8 a.m. he went to get the stolen Fiat 125, while Bompressi headed for the 'area around the home' of Calabresi. There was plenty of time:

Marino stated that he was 'supposed to be near [Calabresi's] main entrance at 8.40 a.m.'. Yet this rendezvous – which, for that matter, Marino fails to keep – has no real meaning. During the trial, '8:40 a.m.' becomes 'ten minutes to nine, more or less, because that was the time that he [Calabresi] would leave the house (more likely, it would be right around 9 a.m.)'.[53]

We can hardly describe Marino as maniacally punctual:

The understanding was that I should be in front of the house from twenty to nine on, as soon as I could. Therefore, it wasn't really necessary [*? Stenographer's note*] for me to be there at twenty to nine or a quarter to nine, or at ten to nine exactly. From twenty to nine on – as soon, let us say, as I was able, according to my own personal judgement, taking into consideration traffic conditions and the availability of parking – I would be there. Let me also point out that in any case, Enrico [i.e. Bompressi] would follow, let us say, my behaviour with the car, and he would automatically be there, ready, as soon as I was ready. I also want to say that if Dottor Calabresi were to leave the house before we were ready, clearly we would try again another day. It wasn't a matter. . . . That is, it wasn't like I had to be there at exactly twenty to nine, otherwise the whole deal was off. I had to be there from twenty to nine on, ready, because Luigi [an unidentified co-conspirator] had told us that he was very likely to leave his house from that time on. (*Trial*, p. 282)

Marino went to the café in the underground station, where he left a beret that Luigi had given him to disguise himself; he got into the Fiat 125; he hit Musicco's Simca and drove off at high speed. According to Musicco's testimony, the accident must have taken place *just after nine* ('five to ten minutes' before the shooting, which took place at 9.12/9.13; *Trial*, pp. 923–4); according to Marino, *immediately after twenty to nine*, when he was still heading for Calabresi's house (*Trial*, p. 282). Marino 'drove around' the area for an unspecified time; at a certain point, he drove along the opposite side of the Via Cherubini, on the even-numbered side, but he could not remember whether, in order to do this, he drove through intersections with stoplights or not (*Trial*, pp. 105–6); he stopped in front of a fruit-and-vegetable stand, located ten metres from Calabresi's residence, and stayed there 'for more than fifteen minutes' with the engine running, pretending to read the paper: 'I had a pistol, which I had placed, let us say, between my legs' (*Trial*, p. 107). Bompressi was waiting for him next to Calabresi's residence and (again according to Marino) had been 'in the area' for more than an hour.[54] These were fairly visible methods of lying in ambush, and one might think that the idea was to be noticed rather than to pass unobserved – yet neither the concierge, nor the owner of the fruit-and-vegetable stand, nor other neighbouring shopkeepers recall the presence of the two assassins. In short, there is a conflict – the twenty minutes separating the accident in the two versions, respectively, of Musicco and Marino – which the presiding judge slides right over, along with a series of remarkably improbable circumstances.

(c) *The car backing up.* 'Almost simultaneously with the shots, in reverse, having previously shifted – wrote Investigating

Magistrate Lombardi in the ordinance-sentence (p. 265) – [Marino] drove backwards for some ten metres, until he reached number 6 in the Via Cherubini', so that Bompressi could get into the car. And the judge commented: 'Only if one had been on the spot could one describe the distances in such detail: . . . that is the approximate distance between the fruit-and-vegetable stand and the building at number 6 in the Via Cherubini.' It is entirely possible that Marino has been in the Via Cherubini at some time in his life; but the car backing up, which he describes repeatedly, entirely eluded the notice of all the eyewitnesses to the murder. When Presiding Judge Minale pointed out this conflict, Marino offered – during the trial – the following explanation (10 January 1990; *Trial*, p. 113, with further reference and explanation on p. 311, 15 January 1990):

I think that I already explained the idea in the previous hearing. In the sense that, when I was backing up, the shots had not yet been fired. The witnesses . . . it is my impression that, in the street, people notice things when there is . . . something noteworthy happens. At the time when I was backing up, no shots had yet been fired, and so nobody noticed (this is my interpretation) the fact that I was backing up. At the very moment that the shots were fired, at that exact moment, I was stopped there, in the middle of the road, so that . . . those who were behind me. . . . Certainly, I was stopped . . . let us say that behind me then . . . those who were behind me were in a line, but it wasn't like I was following them . . .

Marino is floundering; he is tossed a lifesaver:

Presiding judge: 'When you backed up, did you drive in reverse, on a line backwards from your car, in unoccupied space, while there was a line of cars passing on the left, or did you try to enter the line of cars?'

Marino: 'No, I didn't try to enter the line of cars. I backed up . . .'

Presiding judge: 'In this direction, which was unoccupied.'

Marino: 'Yes.'

Presiding judge: 'And why, then, on the other hand, was there this line of cars behind you when you drove off? Because the lines of progress are different. As if there were two tracks. Yours backed up because the street is wide, and then there is the line of cars in motion.'

Marino: 'That I do not know. Probably they had arrived just then.'

This is truly subtle reasoning, but unfortunately, it is roundly contradicted by two very clear eyewitness accounts. On the morning of 17 May 1972, just after 9.10 a.m., the dark-blue Fiat 125, driven by the assassins, was proceeding along the Via Cherubini, followed by an Alfa Romeo 2000, driven by Pietro Pappini, and a Bianchina, driven by Margherita Decio. Immediately after the killing, Pappini described the rapid sequence of events that he witnessed: (1) a very tall man walked out of the main doorway of an apartment building; (2) another very tall man got out of the dark-blue Fiat 125 and crossed the street, came up behind the first man, and fired two shots at him with a pistol, at point-blank range; (3) the shooter crossed the street again and got into the Fiat 125, which then drove off at high speed. Now, according to Pappini's description, the

Fiat 125 was being driven 'very slowly': then, when the shooter got out (event number 2, to which we shall return), the car probably stopped entirely, or almost entirely, since event number 3 was described in the following terms: 'While the man who had been shot was slumping to the ground, [the other man] with the pistol still in his hand was walking backwards to his car, which in the meantime had started up . . .' (29 January 1990; *Trial*, pp. 905–6). The only one who was moving backwards was the shooter; Pappini, even though he was in the best imaginable vantage point, says absolutely nothing about the Fiat 125 backing up. In even more precise terms, Decio stated that she drove along slowly until, after the second pistol shot '(and now I can't say if it was immediately)', the line of cars came to a stop: in particular, one car (the Fiat 125) 'stopped, picked up this person [the shooter], and took off at top speed' (7 February 1990; *Trial*, pp. 1106–7). She, too, makes no mention of a car backing up.

(*d*) *The shooter getting out of and then back into the car.* Tied to the issue of the car backing up is another notable conflict between Marino's account and that of the eyewitnesses: according to Marino, Bompressi had been waiting for some time outside the Calabresi residence; according to the eyewitnesses, the shooter got out of the dark-blue Fiat 125 while Calabresi was crossing the street, then shot him. The ordinance-sentence tended to minimize the importance of this conflict. Presiding Judge Minale took a radically different attitude, at least at first; he pointed out to Marino that: 'the eyewitnesses all seem to agree that there was a single progression: the car moved forward, the killer got out, he followed Dottor Calabresi, shot him, and got back into the car, which was already beginning to move forward . . .' (10 January 1990; *Trial*, p. 112). In reality, the eyewitnesses did not 'all agree', nor was there a 'single progression' – Decio, for instance, said that she did not notice the killer get out of the car. But her view was partly blocked by Pappini's Alfa Romeo 2000. Pappini, on the other hand, who was just behind the dark-blue Fiat 125, stated immediately following the assassination:

> At this point [when the tall man, i.e. Calabresi, was about to cross the street], from the car in question [the dark-blue Fiat 125], I saw a very tall man get out, dressed in a dark-blue jacket and a black high-necked sweater; passing – that is, walking around his car and passing in front of mine – he came up behind the man who had stepped off the pavement, who had, in the meantime, walked from the opposite side of the street and now stood between two automobiles, parked there side by side.

Eighteen years later, this testimony was read in court (29 January 1990). The following exchange ensued (*Trial*, pp. 906–8):

> Presiding judge: 'Are you sure you saw this person get out of the car?'
>
> Pappini: 'The testimony I gave at the time stated that.'
>
> . . .
>
> Presiding judge [*reading the testimony the witness gave in the past*]: ' "While the man who had been shot was slumping to the ground, the shooter, with the pistol still in his hand, was

walking backwards to his car, which in the meantime had started up, getting in and sitting down next to a woman, who was driving."' [*on this detail, see below – Author's note*]

Pappini: 'That I . . . it looked to me like a woman.'

Presiding judge: 'Yes; however, Signor Pappini, we have said that when you heard the shots, you were practically at the intersection with the Via Rasori . . .'

Pappini: 'In the Via Rasori . . . yes.'

Presiding judge: 'There, in the Via Rasori, that is, beyond that false curve . . . [*Stenographer's note: words unclear*]; and what did you see at that moment?'

Pappini: 'The car took off and I saw that gentleman . . . from up . . . that it seemed to me that there was a woman at the wheel.'

Presiding judge: 'And where was the car? Still in front of you?'

Pappini: 'Yes, it was right in front of me.'

Presiding judge: 'And this gentleman that got in, where did he come from?'

Pappini: 'From where the murder took place . . . from where they killed that man.'

Presiding judge: 'Yes, but you, right then, you didn't know where the killing had taken place: you knew nothing and you heard two shots.'

Pappini: 'I heard the shots and that was it.'

Presiding judge: 'And so, why do you say that he came from the killing?'

Pappini: 'Because he walked in front of me and he wasn't even running: that gentleman was walking slowly.'

Presiding judge: 'Yes, but how can you say that this was the same person who got out of the car?'

Pappini: 'I . . . perhaps when I looked back, or something – I don't know – or hearing two shots, which I had never heard before, perhaps . . .'

Presiding judge: 'You heard two shots and you drove off to one side, you said.'

Pappini: 'When you are afraid . . . [*Stenographer's note: voices overlapping*] . . . The fear caused me to go . . .'

Presiding judge: 'Therefore, you weren't looking back.'

Pappini: 'I wasn't looking back.'

Presiding judge: 'So, how can you say that the person who got out was the same person who later got back into the car?'

Pappini: 'I don't know . . . I really can't remember any more. I don't even remember any more.'

Presiding judge [*reading*]: '"The shooter, before climbing into the car, hid the pistol in an inside pocket of his jacket . . ."'

Pappini: 'Yes, that guy, I saw him get into the whatsit and hide the pistol.'

Presiding judge [*continuing to read*]: '". . . and then they took off in the direction of the Via Mario Pagano." The individual who fired – you say – was "roughly 1.76/1.8 metres in height, of average build, wore no hat, with dark wavy hair, about thirty years old, good-looking, with a dark-blue jacket and a dark high-necked sweater.": that is what you said. Now, the description you gave – who is that? Is it the person you saw get out of the car, or is it the person you saw get in, or the shooter (whom you should not have seen)?'

Pappini: 'Either it was the person who got out, or else the person who got in . . . I no longer remember.'

Presiding judge: 'Yes; but you said "the shooter", but you
– you didn't see the shooter.'

Pappini: 'No, no, I heard the shots.'

Presiding judge: 'You heard the shots; then – the person
whose description you gave, who is that?'

Pappini: 'Of that man who got into the car.'

Presiding judge: 'The one who got in and put the pistol
into his . . .'

Pappini [*Stenographer's note: answer incomprehensible due to
voices overlapping*]: '. . . in the car.'

Presiding judge: 'And do you remember if that was the
same person who got out?'

Pappini: 'No, I didn't notice.'

Presiding judge: 'And so – you didn't even remember?'

Pappini: 'Didn't even?'

Presiding judge: 'Back then.'

Pappini: 'No, no, no, I really don't remember.'

I have never met Signor Pappini. I did not attend the trial in
which he appeared as a witness. From the transcripts I read,
it appears that he was born in 1932 in Cornaredo, in the prov-
ince of Milan; nothing more. The Alfa 2000 that he was driving
that morning in May 1972 suggests that he was well-to-do;
perhaps a businessman. I have a footnote, inserted, in this and
in other cases, by the stenographer: 'The transcription of the
testimony of the witness is complete, including the interjections
in dialect and the slang expressions, and may therefore be difficult to read at certain points.' I found it perfectly eloquent. A
judge, pressing and plying with questions, insisting, swinging
sophistries through the air like so many sabres, using his own

power and knowledge to the utmost . . . where (I wondered as I read the exchanges between Presiding Judge Minale and Signor Pappini) have I already seen all this? It may be a result of the work I do, but I could not help thinking – once again – of a trial held by the Inquisition: one of those witch trials in which the inquisitor gradually manages to convince a defendant that the Virgin Mary who appeared to her was actually the Devil; that the nocturnal 'parties' in which another defendant says he participates in spirit are actually the Black Sabbath, and so on.[55] Here, instead, we have a judge and a witness rather than a judge and a defendant; but today, just as in the past, those who possess more power and more knowledge try (in perfect good faith, let us be clear) to persuade others to come over to their point of view. What is at stake is something quite fragile: a handful of perceptions, impressed eighteen years before on the memory of an individual. Like many other witnesses to the killing, Pappini saw a man get out of a dark-blue car, shoot, and get back into the same car. He saw this, perhaps, more clearly than anyone else, since when the man got out of the car he walked right in front of the Alfa Romeo 2000 that Pappini was driving. In the face of the press of doubts and pedantic distinctions formulated by the presiding judge, however, Pappini begins to waver: his certainty about what he had seen just a few metres away eighteen years before gradually crumbles. The shooter splits into the person who got out of the car and the person who got into the car; then he becomes another person, different from those two; finally he dissolves. The testimony given immediately following the killing, when his memory was clear, crumbles in retrospect: 'And so – you didn't even remember?' 'Didn't even?' 'Back then.' 'No, no, no,

I really don't remember.' But his uncertainty is only temporary. When, a few minutes later, the presiding judge starts in again, Pappini stands firm:

Presiding judge: 'Why do you say that the person who got out of the car is the same person who, then, got into the car later?'

Pappini: 'For the simple reason that, on that day. . . . OK, now I am talking about that day. . . . That person who got out of the car – I saw him get back into the car, when I heard the shots; I think that it was him, in short . . .'

Presiding judge: 'That is, you remember seeing the same person.'

Pappini: 'To me, yes, it was the same person.'

The witness was allowed to go.

(e) *The woman at the wheel.* On this point, let us listen once again to the testimony of Pappini (*Trial*, pp. 906–11):

Presiding judge [*reading the testimony the witness gave in the past*]: ' "While the man who had been shot was slumping to the ground, the shooter, with the pistol still in his hand, was walking backwards to his car, which in the meantime had started up, getting in and sitting down next to a woman, who was driving." '

Pappini: 'That I . . . it looked to me like a woman.'

. . .

Pappini: 'The car took off and I saw that gentleman . . . from up . . . that it seemed to me that there was a woman at the wheel.'

. . .

Presiding judge: 'Then, you say: [*reading the testimony that the witness gave in the past*]: "The woman who was at the wheel of the Fiat 125, I saw her from behind, and so I could not describe her, but in any case she had chestnut hair, smooth, with a hairdo that presented from one side ... [*Stenographer's note: word pronounced badly*] towards the outside, and on the other side smooth." Now, this is the question: was the woman at the wheel the woman driving the car from which you saw this person get out ...?'

Pappini: 'Yes.'

Presiding judge: '... and not the person who was driving the car into which he got afterwards?'

[Now the sleight of hand has taken on dizzying proportions: before our very eyes, not only have two shooters materialized – one getting out of the car, the other getting into it – but even two women and two cars. Hats off, Judge Minale! Pappini appears somewhat befuddled, but he does not yield.]

Pappini: 'No, from the one that person got out of, I think ... I think so ... which, to my mind, was a woman who.... When the car took off ... which I saw, because I – in my car – I went to the right, and, when the car took off fast ... to me, I saw and it looked to me like a woman, in short.'

Presiding judge: 'Yes – no, I wanted to ask you in greater detail: when you talk about a woman, are you referring to the "woman who was at the wheel of the car that was in front of you, and which this gentleman got out of?"'

Pappini: 'Yes, yes ... the car that was in front of me.'

Presiding judge: 'And on the other hand, who was driving the car that the gentleman got into, and then put the pistol in his pocket – did you see who was driving?'

Pappini: 'A woman, to my mind.'

Presiding judge: 'That was a woman too?'

Pappini: 'Yes, to my mind it was a woman.'

Presiding judge: 'And you had the impression that it was the same woman?'

Pappini: 'I think so, because if the car was in front of me, and I was going slowly, when I heard the shots and I veered off to the right . . . it was still that same car, which drove off fast along the Via Rasori.'

Presiding judge: 'And why do you talk about a woman?'

Pappini: 'Because, looking up, it seemed like a woman to me.'

. . .

Presiding judge: 'Then you said, at the time: "If I were to see this person with the pistol again, I would be able to recognize him"; and today, what do you remember about this person?'

Pappini: 'In fact, they showed me two or three people one evening, in the Via Moscova, and I did not recognize them; in fact, I said it wasn't them, immediately.'

Presiding judge: 'But did they show you a woman?'

Pappini: 'They also showed me a little short woman . . . but the woman was sitting at the wheel: how could I have seen her?'

Presiding judge: 'When they showed you a woman to see if you recognized her, did that puzzle you?'

Pappini: 'No, I immediately said that I did not recognize her.'

Presiding judge: 'No, what I mean is: were you puzzled about the fact, and did you say: "Why are you showing me a

woman? I am not sure whether it was a woman or a man?",
or did this fact not puzzle you at all?'

[A fine example of a leading question, modestly concealed
by the feeble closing alternative. Likewise, in times less enlight-
ened than our own, unscrupulous judges would coerce weak-
willed or frightened defendants. Once again, however, Pappini
could not be intimidated.]

Pappini: 'No, no, I don't think that I was puzzled at all.'

Presiding judge: 'Which is to say, to your mind, it actually
had been a woman?'

Pappini: 'To my mind, it actually had been a woman.'

Presiding judge: 'And what factors led you to this belief?'

Pappini: 'The long hair that the person had.'

Other eyewitnesses had had the same impression or, in other
cases, the same doubt. Let us begin with a case that is in many
ways anomalous: that of Adelia Dal Piva. On the morning of
the assassination, she was leaving a bank branch office located
in the Via Ariosto, where she had just finished paying her
phone bill. Suddenly she saw a dark-blue Fiat 125 pull up at
high speed. She then saw 'a man and a woman, and specifically,
the woman from the driver's side' get out of the car, and she
saw them only from behind. Dal Piva did not realize until a
few days later that this car was the one that had been used by
Calabresi's killers: and she did not go to the police until 30
May 1972. The initial police report drawn up on that occasion
contains, apart from a brief reference to the clothing worn by
the man (matching the clothing worn by the shooter), a very
detailed description of the clothing worn by the woman who
had been driving the dark-blue Fiat 125:

She was dressed in black: in fact, more specifically, she was wearing a pair of black trousers (I cannot remember whether they were corduroy or some other material), a light sleeveless, collarless jacket that reached down to the top of her thighs; extending from beneath the light jacket were the sleeves of an article of clothing, red in colour; I could not clearly determine whether it was a blouse or a light sweater. With reference to the above description, I would add that I recall that the light jacket was a little shorter than would have been appropriate to the woman's build; in fact, her rotundity caught the eye of the observer as one of the salient details of this woman, at least when seen from behind.

And Dal Piva added: 'In describing the young woman, I forgot to mention the colour and the length of her hair: it reached her shoulders, and it seemed to me that it rested on her shoulders; golden blonde in colour (not the colour of a pale person, a richer blonde).'

The duo then boarded an Alfa Romeo Giulia, which was waiting with a man at the wheel. The woman sat next to the driver; the man who boarded with her sat in the back seat. At the sound of an approaching police car, the Giulia took off. Before it did so, however, Dal Piva declared, the woman took:

in her hand a round mirror, and looking into it, she said something, of which I heard distinctly the following exact phrases: 'Stupid, don't move ... go (or stay) straight ... we will cover you (or we will pick you up or we will accompany you).' The woman – let me repeat – was sitting with her back held quite erect and facing straight ahead, and looked into the mirror as she said these words, without moving her face either left or back, so that I could not understand which of the two men she was speaking to; indeed, I thought that she was speaking to someone outside the car by means of a radio transmitter hidden in the mirror. In this context, I had an opportunity to look at the woman's profile: she had a full, round cheek – that is, one could tell that she was not a thin woman – and an average nose. The cheek that I could see was not covered by her hair. Let me state that I was able to see her right cheek. . . . The detail of this woman that most struck me was her walk, which I cannot describe but would certainly recognize.

Eighteen years later, Dal Piva stated in her testimony that she remembered very little: the car arriving at high speed, the two people getting out: 'one . . . rather plump, let us say, and it seemed like a woman to me (because I could not see their faces), and the other one who got out . . . a man, skinny, tall.' Then, gradually, as her old statement was read back to her, she confirmed nearly everything. She had no recollection at all of the words pronounced into the mirror; in retrospect, she gave the scene a more ordinary interpretation ('I thought she might be applying make-up'). She did confirm her impression of the female identity of the 'little plump one', repeatedly disputed by the presiding judge: 'How can you tell from behind? From behind, it seemed like a woman to me . . . and an unsightly woman, in short, stout and short.' The hair, she added, made her think of a wig (*Trial*, pp. 945–58).

The quaint conjecture concerning the radio transmitter hidden in the mirror should be clearly distinguished from the testimony proper: it is difficult to imagine that the woman seen – and so minutely described – by Dal Piva was a man rather than a woman. A foolish stereotype, on the other hand, led Antonio Zanicchi – who had been in the Via Cherubini at the moment of the killing – to reject his first, unreflecting impression (*Trial*, p. 901). He had seen 'through the glass [of the Fiat 125], because I was there . . . that it seemed as if he wore a wig or, at any rate, was blond, and noticed the way he put the car in gear and took off, and I thought to myself: "It can't be a woman, he drives so well" . . . and these were things more typical . . . that a man could do, rather than a woman. . . .' Another witness, Luciano Gnappi (20 February 1990; *Trial*, p. 1673), had been puzzled as he looked at the person driving the dark-blue Fiat 125: he had noticed 'the long hair: in fact, I almost had the feeling that it was a woman, then, however, I said . . . these days, there were hippies already, so it could also have been a man with long hair'. When, however, lawyer Gentili asked him, during the trial, whether the driver's long hair 'was long and straight, or bushy', Gnappi was quite clear: 'No . . . bushy hair – I would rule that out. The hair was long and slightly wavy, like . . . I don't know . . . a woman's almost . . . [*Stenographer's note: audio too low*] a little straighter, at least as far as I am concerned.'

The significance of Gentili's questions is quite clear. Marino had – and has – long thick hair: 'bushy, in other words', as he described it himself (10 January 1990; *Trial*, pp. 127–8). If it had been possible to identify him as the woman driving the car, seen or hypothesized by so many eyewitnesses, his version would remain intact, though wobbly – it would remain unclear, in fact, why he never mentioned wearing a wig during the assassination. If, however, it really was a woman driving the dark-blue Fiat 125, then Marino's version collapses. (It is worth noting that a woman, Gudrun Kiess, was jailed because she was suspected of being the driver in the assassination, though she did not even have a driving licence.) During the preliminary inquest, Marino declared: 'I read in the newspapers reports of a blonde woman having taken part in the killing, or a person with a wig like that, but that is absolutely impossible, since neither Enrico [i.e. Bompressi] nor I had wigs, and Enrico did not have long blond hair. I remember that when I read those reports I thought the police had deliberately leaked this information in order to confuse us about the progress of the investigation' (25 July 1988; *Preliminary Inquest*, p. 23).

We know that this last supposition is not accurate. Why should Marino's version carry more weight than all of the testimony cited, taken as a whole?

We might add that the police found, in the dark-blue Fiat 125 used in the assassination, a black retractable umbrella, but also a cheap pair of woman's sunglasses: both of unknown origin. At the preliminary inquest, Marino, who remembered neither of these articles, did not rule out the possibility that the sunglasses might have been those he had been given by Luigi (the mysterious accomplice), which he had then put into the pocket of his jacket. He said, however (and confirmed in court), that he had forgotten what these sunglasses looked like: 'I do not remember the exact appearance of these glasses, in part because, in fact, as I said, I never actually used them. I put them in my pocket and then I did not use them, so I absolutely do not remember what . . .' (10 January 1990; *Trial*, p. 103). A remarkable oversight, given that the sunglasses were 'strikingly feminine' (to quote a police report on record, cited by lawyer Gentili: *Trial*, p. 313).

(*f*) *The retractable umbrella.* In the investigations conducted following the murder of Calabresi, it was discovered that an umbrella like the one found in the dark-blue Fiat 125 had been sold four days before, on the afternoon of 13 May, in a Standa department store. The salesperson clearly remembered the person who had asked her to explain how the umbrella worked (the only umbrella of its type sold that day) before he purchased it. An Identikit, which was immediately and widely distributed, was developed from the salesperson's description. Here is that description: 'He was about 1.75 metres tall; slender build; straight blond hair, combed back, with a tuft of hair in the centre that was slightly more reddish than the rest of his hair; rosy complexion; long face; thin lips; rather large ears; he wore a dark suit; he spoke Italian with a foreign accent . . . but I could not say what nationality. I had the impression that the tuft of hair and the rest of his hair had been dyed.'

This last detail, just like the detail of the hair 'combed back', played an important role in the trial that followed as a result of Marino's confessions. Marino claimed that on 20 May he had travelled with Laura Vigliardi Paravia to Massa, where Sofri, just before the rally (the first following the death of Calabresi), congratulated him on the work he had done. On the same occasion, Marino claimed to have noticed 'that Bompressi had slightly changed his hairstyle (the way he wore his hair) . . . and his hair was also, let us say, a little lighter in colour than usual ... like someone who had just gone to the barber and who has, let us say, a different way of wearing his hair from how he usually wears it; in short ... [Laura Vigliardi Paravia] said to me ... : "Did you see what he did to his hair? Now, he looks even more like the Identikit, in other words"' (*Trial*, p. 125).

But Marino's account, just like the fully convergent account of Antonia Bistolfi, is absolutely improbable; and not only because the alleged tinting of Bompressi's hair had completely escaped the notice of both Bompressi's friends in Massa and Police Superintendent Costantino (*Trial*, pp. 1284, 1293, 1302, 1357, etc.). The fact is that the purchaser of the umbrella and the shooter were (as was evident from eyewitness descriptions) two different people; the police recognized that their identity was different, and in fact two different Identikits were constructed (actually, one photofit and one Identikit); the detail of the tinted hair referred to the man who bought the umbrella, not the shooter; on the afternoon of 13 May, however, Bompressi (who was not only much taller than the unknown buyer of the umbrella, but speaks Italian with a Massa accent, not a foreign accent) could not have purchased an umbrella in Milan because he was attending a rally in Pisa at which Sofri was speaking.

As we have seen, the account of the killing of Calabresi given by Marino contains a vast number of improbable or unacceptable details. The mistake concerning the colour of the car may certainly be described as a 'minor error', to use the words of Investigating Magistrate Lombardi. When, however, we come to the crash with Musicco's car, the shooter who gets out of the car instead of waiting outside Calabresi's residence, the blond hair (natural or tinted) of the driver – man or woman – of the dark-blue Fiat 125, we can no longer speak of errors, major or minor. We are forced to conclude that, in all likelihood, Marino is lying about the killing of Calabresi.

XVI

I do not know what pushed Marino to lie. The psychological motivations underlying his lies seem to me, however, to be wholly irrelevant in this context. I know perfectly well that summations by prosecuting counsel, speeches to the court by defence lawyers, and judgements of every sort and level all overflow with psychological motivations, usually of the very lowest order. But that sort of psychology (which even historians are, by now, ashamed to use) should be banished from courtrooms everywhere. It only encourages incontrovertible affirmations, which can be used to demonstrate everything and the opposite of everything.

Let us take the case of Marino. Judge Lombardi's ordinance-sentence emphasized – as has been pointed out above – Marino's profound disgust with the crimes he had committed, his authentic remorse, his 'ethical' nature. Lombardi's prose is rhetorical and hollow; the effort to turn Marino into a latter-day Raskolnikov is laughable. The words used by Marino to describe his own remorse are slovenly, stereotypical: not only at the preliminary inquest, where they reach us through a bureaucratic filter, but in court as well. Yet what importance can we attribute to these indicators of inauthenticity? Absolutely none. Psychological intuitions, just like the 'gut reactions' so abjectly evoked by Assistant District Attorney Pomarici in his summation, have absolutely no probative worth.[56] A far different – and greater – weight can be assigned to the errors, the inconsistencies, and the contradictions that spangle Marino's version.

During the course of the trial, as we have noted, the official version of Marino's repentance and confession crumbled into dust. Before the end of the trial, the presiding judge summoned Marino for a final interrogation, urging him to speak sincerely at last. Why had he concealed his meetings with the *carabinieri*? What had persuaded him to repent and confess? Once again, we hear of the meetings between Marino and the parish priest of Bocca di Magra, mentioned at the beginning of the trial. We hear again of the threats that Marino attributed at first to un-identified former accomplices in terrorist acts, and later to a simple misunderstanding on the part of the parish priest. And now, after much aimless talk and numerous digressions, a third version emerged. Here it is.

Marino would go from time to time to Turin, where his mother and sisters lived. During the early months of 1987, in a bar frequented by former comrades, he had run into Renzo Marauda, who had suggested that they rob the RAI (Italian state-run television and radio) headquarters, where Marauda worked as a messenger (*Trial*, p. 2159). During the preliminary inquest, Marino had already minutely described the plan and its failure. The expected take was of the order of 800 million lire. Marino would have been given 100 million lire. He had accepted Marauda's plan in part because 'in that period he was entering a time of economic hardship' (*Preliminary Inquest*, pp. 29–31). During the trial, he explained that he purchased an old truck from a vendor for 5 million lire, which he had paid in instalments. In the summer of 1987 he had sold crêpes: but towards August the town police had begun to fine him because he was parking the truck in an illegal spot in a limited-parking zone. He had also sold crêpes during the following winter; at times he would drive the truck to neighbouring towns, when there were fairs. Once or twice, Marauda had come to see him (in spring 1988; he was not sure when) in Bocca di Magra, urging him to make a second stab at the unsuccessful hold-up at RAI. Marino had not refused point-blank; but the failure of the previous year had scared him; he had children now, and he was beginning to feel too old for this sort of thing. One day, a town policeman came to see him and told him that he could not park his truck there any more: 'If you go on parking here, we will have to make a report to the local police magistrate.' In short, they were making it impossible for him to work. During the same period, his landlord had demanded a resort-level rent from him (2.6 million lire) for the two summer months in the beach town. He had threatened to evict Marino if he did not pay; the landlord had even sent a lawyer to talk to Marino. Marino said:

> I told him that I had no intention of paying and that in any case I didn't have the money to pay, so that he shouldn't ... that he could do what he wanted. And so, these two things are two things that happened almost at the same time; in other words, in that same period. So – this is what I meant to say before, when I said that it is difficult for me to say what happened in my head, for me to make a decision of this sort. I remember that that

> morning I no longer knew what to do, in the sense that I
> ... because I didn't ... I got in my car and I drove around
> all morning ... I didn't know who to talk to and at a certain
> point I found myself in front of the *carabinieri* barracks and
> I went in and from that moment on, you see, I started to
> ... (*Trial*, pp. 2164–5)

Philosophers, poets and novelists have taught us that the heart
is driven by reasons that reason cannot understand; that the
human soul is often contradictory; that momentous decisions
are sometimes made in a hasty, brusque fashion, after a hidden,
sometimes unconscious struggle. Marino's story is absurd, and
therefore psychologically plausible. But no one can say whether
it is true, partly true and partly false, or completely false. As I
write these words (10 November 1990), the written judgement,
which was required to be published within sixty days of the
court's decision, has yet to be seen. I can imagine the author
of that work, responsible for this scandalous delay, as he con-
structs a psychological portrait of Marino, based on the passage
I have just cited. Instead of the scraps of *Crime and Punishment*
that Lombardi foisted upon us, perhaps we shall read some by-
product of Camus's *The Outsider*. Plausibility, however (including the psychological plausibility of the absurd), is not the same
as truth. Just what was passing through Marino's mind as he
entered – for the first time, according to his story – the *carabinieri* barracks in Ameglia? Remorse, desire for vindication,
expectations of material gain – who can say?

'In other words', the presiding judge had asked at the
beginning of the trial, 'if you had found the money, you would
have continued the same sort of life, and you would have found

some way of lulling your conscience, wouldn't you?' (*Trial*, p. 28).

Almost three months later came Marino's reply:

... if you are asking me whether in other situations I wouldn't ... have made the decision to confess, I answer with great honesty that I cannot say, and perhaps I would not have, or perhaps I would have: and now there is no way to say, in the sense that, if I had won the National Lottery and become a billionaire, perhaps I would not have felt this necessity, or else I might have felt it just the same, and that I cannot say. (*Trial*, p. 2178)

Fear, threats, attempts to draw him back into a life of crime by Marauda: the presiding judge had tried for the umpteenth time to make sense of this muddle.

Marino: 'I don't know what you are trying to say: but if you intend to say that I – let us say – might have decided to confess, not out of remorse and a sense of conscience, but for other reasons, this ...'

Presiding judge: 'No, no ... I am not saying that.' (*Trial*, p. 2177)

XVII

In all likelihood, Marino is lying; certainly Marino was believed to be telling the truth. The trial of Adriano Sofri and his fellow defendants ended, in the lower court, in a judicial error. I say error, because to speak of criminal intent (which in this case would also necessarily imply a conspiracy) one must have solid evidence. I have no such evidence. Concerning the fact, however, that first the investigating magistrates, and subsequently the judges of the Milan Court of Assizes, led astray by Marino's false confessions, committed an error, there can, I think, be no doubt.

To err, of course, is human. But for a judge – just as for anyone who is professionally involved in the search for truth – error is not merely a risk: it is a dimension in which one is constantly immersed. Not only is human knowledge intrinsically fallible: it progresses through error: attempting, erring, correcting itself. Error and truth imply one another, like shadow and light. Now, not all errors have equal consequences. There are catastrophic errors, innocuous errors, fecund errors. In the judicial sphere, however, this last category cannot exist. Judicial error, even when it is reversible, inevitably translates into a dead loss for justice.

I mention these obvious truths in order to cast light on the implications of the comparison – suggested above – between Presiding Judge Minale's attitude towards certain witnesses and the attitude of certain inquisitors during witch trials. The Inquisition, as an institution, is abhorrent to me – a judgement that has nothing to do with the moral and intellectual qualities of its functionaries. One can only suppose that among those functionaries there were scrupulous individuals, just as there were intelligent, ferocious and idiotic individuals (and these qualities often coexist, simultaneously or at different times, in the same person). For nearly two centuries, however, this presumable variety of individual qualities seems to have been contradicted by a recurring tendency to examine cases of witchcraft by working from hypotheses that were virtually impossible to disprove. The literature of demonology taught, for example, that if a suspected witch were to confess, she was guilty; if she remained silent, even under torture, she did so by virtue of an enchantment (the so-called *maleficium taciturnitatis*); if she denied being a witch, then she lied, seduced by the Devil, father of lies. Such reasoning as this presupposed innocence or guilt in each case, rather than setting out to demonstrate innocence or guilt. In all likelihood, such reasoning encouraged whatever propensity an inquisitor might have to use his power to extract or exact – most of the time, in absolute good faith – confessions from the accused within pre-existing frameworks.

The more one eludes the possibility of disproving one's theory, the more one remains vulnerable to error. This obvious correlation is strikingly evident to anyone who, today, reads transcripts of most of the witch trials held in Europe between the fifteenth and seventeenth centuries. The crude retrospective evaluation set forth in the text mentioned, *Instructio pro formandis processibus in causis strigum*, presupposed a consideration of this sort. The anonymous author of that text – certainly someone who moved in the circle of the Roman Congregation of the Holy Office (or Inquisition) – asked that the inquisitors of the outlying courts seek evidence: objective corroboration, as we might say nowadays.

Judge Lombardi's ordinance-sentence speaks of an 'enormous array of objective corroboration acquired during the course of the preliminary inquest', making it possible to 'formulate with a clear conscience a judgement of complete reliability upon Marino's statements'. This 'reliability', however (and this is the point), must be extended – the ordinance-sentence goes on – to the part, as well, 'in which he [Marino] offers information that cannot be borne out by external corroboration'. Before we examine the principle according to which this procedure is justified, we should emphasize that the 'information' to which Lombardi is alluding includes decisive elements of the prosecution's case, especially everything concerning conversations with the alleged instigators. Marino claims, in fact, that he spoke with them alone, and without witnesses: with Pietrostefani repeatedly in Turin; with Sofri in Pisa, immediately after the speech Sofri delivered during a rally on 13 May 1972, on the pavement in front of a café. This circumstance was later decisively rejected in court by numerous witnesses, including Guelfo Guelfi, a Lotta Continua militant who – following Sofri's speech and the short discussion that ensued over the proposal to erect a plaque dedicated to Franco Serantini immediately – drove with Sofri to the house of a mutual friend, Soriano Ceccanti (*Trial*, pp. 1516–20). Guelfi is a friend of Sofri: is this a sufficient reason to take Marino's word rather than his?

The ordinance-sentence continues as follows: 'Even such indications [unsupported by objective corroboration] should be considered adequate sources of proof against the defendants thus implicated; in fact they fit persuasively, in logical and chronological terms, within the probatory framework, rich in corroborative elements, laid out hitherto.' That would be 'completely in keeping with present-day jurisprudential orientation, which requires, for accusations of shared complicity, some form of concrete corroboration or at least evidence of internal consistency to the statements, even if they refer to different periods of time'. At this point, the ordinance-sentence anticipates a potential objection: 'Certainly, what is commonly stated in jurisprudential terms with reference to the so-called "fallacy of generalization" is true enough; therefore the veracity of statements that have been ascertained to be accurate on certain points does not automatically extend to all the other points.' Still, this recognition is only apparent: 'it is, however, also an accepted principle', the ordinance-sentence goes on, 'that the reliability of the statements must be *evaluated overall, as a whole*; that reliability, therefore, reflects on the entire array of material placed before the Magistrate for examination, when one is dealing with a matter *possessing intrinsic and monolithic features that are logically indivisible*'.

Just what the words I have put in italics actually mean is not clear. Judge Lombardi, however, immediately offers an explanation:

This means that if John Doe makes statements that can be ascertained to be true concerning three separate crimes with which one or more persons can be charged, this does not automatically mean that he has also told the truth concerning a fourth crime, entirely different and not connected with the previous ones, involving the same or other individuals; if, on the other hand, a defendant makes statements concerning a matter with monolithic features, the external objective corroborative elements that may be discovered concerning several of the specific acts will also produce their effects in relation to other acts which those proven acts presuppose or which follow those acts as an inevitable consequence.

The 'matter possessing intrinsic and monolithic features' has now become a 'matter with monolithic features'; the expression 'logically indivisible' now refers to acts 'which those proven acts presuppose or which follow those acts as an inevitable consequence'. We have now entered, as the reader may clearly see, the realm of the purest and most insolent tautology. Behind these verbose reiterations, however, are concealed declarations with quite concrete consequences.

The expression 'logically indivisible', which follows the 'matter possessing intrinsic and monolithic features', probably refers to the so-called 'logical proof' mentioned immediately afterwards by the ordinance-sentence. This form of proof is defined as follows: in accusations of complicity, the facts that are recounted must be 'compatible with the generally known information that has already been established, both concerning the criminal acts in question and concerning the normal behavioural reactions of the individuals involved in this sort of act' (*Ordinance-Sentence*, pp. 107–8).[57] This means, in the case we are examining here, that if (1) the robberies that Marino claims to have taken part in are proven; if (2) some of them were committed, according to Marino, on behalf of the so-called illegal group within Lotta Continua; then (3) Marino's confessions concerning the order to kill Calabresi issued by the so-called executive committee and (4) concerning the role played in instigating this killing by Pietrostefani and Sofri may be accepted without any objective corroboration.

This is the line being pursued – unless I am mistaken – in a comment by Armando Spataro, assistant district attorney of the Republic in Milan, concerning the first verdict delivered by the Milan Court of Assizes. The statement was made in an interview published in the magazine *Società Civile* (June 1990). Spataro states that he followed the trial closely, participating in a couple of interrogations and supporting the decisions made by his office and by the chief district attorney, Borrelli. This comment, therefore, carried particular authority. Spataro emphasizes 'the results of the investigation in that mountainous or hilly area in Piedmont where, according to Marino, the clandestine group within Lotta Continua conducted its target practice'. The former landlord of an abandoned farmhouse mentioned in Marino's testimony, Spataro states:

> . . . told investigators that at the time he had found human silhouettes drawn on the walls with bullet holes in them. . . . This may seem like a marginal confirmation. Instead, it is fundamental. Because it proves the existence of a clandestine group within Lotta Continua. And because, once you have demonstrated the fact that Marino and Bompressi took part in the killing, the next step is that responsibility is necessarily attributed to a specific group with a political leadership. And for that matter, why did the other defendants' line of defence focus on denying Marino's culpability? Any experienced lawyer would sense that this was a theory, a desperate ploy. It ought to have been easier to show simply that one's client was not involved, and say: Marino may well have been involved, but with who-knows-whom. But that is not what they did. Because once you have demonstrated that Marino was involved, everything else follows of necessity.

'Which is to say?' inquires the interviewer, Nando Dalla Chiesa. 'That it is unthinkable,' continues Spataro, 'that Marino, a member of a clandestine group that truly did exist, should have acted on his own, on his own initiative, committing the first political homicide in the 1970s, exposing his organization in such a way. And note this: there is plenty of proof of the existence of the clandestine group: documents, weapons, and all the rest.' 'Isn't this stretching it a bit?' asks Dalla Chiesa. 'Not at all,' responds Spataro. 'Consider this: logical reasoning is the most solid part of any judicial decision – and not in this case alone, but in the everyday administration of justice. To say that two plus two equals four is legitimate; there is no need to find a citation for the number four. And in this case, that is what we have.'

In his response, which appeared in the subsequent issue of the same magazine, Adriano Sofri demonstrates the nonexistence of the alleged 'objective corroboration' cited by Spataro. In both cases (because Spataro carelessly confuses two places mentioned by Marino, Corio nel Canavese and a farmhouse in the Novara area[58]) nothing solid was found; the vague recollections of an elderly former partner of a long-ago tenant were contradicted in court by the daughter of the former tenant and by a lance-corporal in the *carabinieri*; and so on and so forth. These factual results are important. I would like to focus more specifically, however, on questions of method: in part because the assistant district attorney's reasoning processes are in line with those used by the investigating magistrate and (admittedly with some oscillations) by the presiding judge of the Court of Assizes.

Let us immediately dispense with the reference to 'two plus

two equals four'. It is entirely uncalled for. While 'four' *necessarily* follows 'two plus two' (and in this sense there is no need to find it written down), so-called 'logical proof' speaks of *compatibility* ('compatible with the generally known information already acquired, etc.'). Even a child understands the difference; perhaps an assistant district attorney should understand it as well.

Is it legitimate, then, to substitute – for objective corroboration of an individual's behaviour – undocumented information, which is merely *compatible* with the facts that have actually been ascertained? We must distinguish between political legitimacy and logical legitimacy. Let us begin with political legitimacy. According to Nando Dalla Chiesa (whom we have just seen interviewing Assistant District Attorney Spataro), those who denounce the abuse of 'logical proof' are underestimating the gravity of the situation created by the growing weight – political weight, as well – of organized crime in Italy.[59] In trials of the Mafia and the Camorra, reliance upon 'logical proof' becomes necessary in dealing with individuals who destroy, conceal, or alter evidence. This reasoning troubles me, even though I have no doubt about the decisive importance of the struggle against organized crime. In any case, this is an approach that can hardly be used in a radically different sort of trial, such as the trial of the alleged killers of Calabresi. Here, we see the simultaneous triumph of 'logical proof' and the destruction of physical evidence (the victim's clothing, the car used by the killers, the fatal bullet) – a destruction that can scarcely be attributed to the defendants.

Let us now attempt to answer the question asked above (the integration of objective corroboration based on compatible

tion) in logical terms. We thus return to the question hich we initially set out: the question of the relationship judge and historian. The answer – all appearances aside – is less than obvious.

XVIII

Judge and historian, as we have said, are linked by the shared belief that it is possible to 'prove, according to given rules, that x did y: where x may equally well indicate the protagonist (perhaps nameless) of a historic event or the subject of a penal proceeding; and y an action of any sort'.[60] This convergence, however, is valid only in abstract terms: if we examine the way in which judges and historians work, we will discover a profound divergence. For a long time, in fact, historians have focused almost exclusively on political and military events: on states, not individuals. And states, unlike individuals, cannot be prosecuted under the law.

The study of individual lives dates back to the Ancient Greeks. In a series of lectures delivered at Harvard in 1968, later published under the title *The Development of Greek Biography*, Arnaldo Momigliano insisted on the distinction between the two literary genres, history and biography.[61] That distinction was long-lived. One can write the biography of Alcibiades, Cesare Borgia, or Mirabeau – the great nineteenth-century German historian Droysen once observed – but not that of Caesar, or Frederick the Great. 'The adventurer, the failure, the marginal figure,' commented Momigliano, 'were the subjects for biography.'[62] The lives of those whom Hegel called 'world-historical individuals',[63] rather, are entirely one with universal history.

The nineteenth century, on the other hand, was not merely the century of Napoleon. It was also the century that witnessed the complete triumph of the bourgeoisie, the transformation of the European countryside, unbridled urbanization, the first labour struggles, and the beginning of the emancipation of women. A historical analysis of these phenomena presupposed an updating of the conceptual, technical and stylistic tools of traditional historiography. What, however, would eventually be called social history, the offspring of the eighteenth-century *histoire des mœurs*, developed only piecemeal, step by step. Oddly, an early manifesto of history 'from below', written by the author of the famous *Essai sur l'histoire de la formation et du progrès du Tiers État* (1850), Augustin Thierry, appeared in the form of an 'imaginary biography'. It was a very short essay entitled *Histoire véritable de Jacques Bonhomme, d'après des documents authentiques* (1820): a life of Jacques the peasant, extending over twenty centuries, from the Roman invasion to the present. It was, of course, a 'jest', even though Thierry was clearly using the single protagonist to emphasize a doleful conclusion: the conquerors might change (Romans, Franks, absolute monarchy, republic, empire, constitutional monarchy); the forms of domination might change; but the dominion over the peasants, generation after generation, remained unchanged. The same narrative approach was used by Michelet in the first part of *La Sorcière* (1862); here the metamorphosis and subterranean continuity of witchcraft are depicted through the figure of a woman, the Witch, who comprises the events of many centuries. It seems clear to me that Michelet took his inspiration from Thierry.[64] In both cases the intention was to salvage, through a symbolic character, a multitude of lives crushed by poverty and oppression – the lives of those who, as Baudelaire put it in an unforgettable verse, 'n'ont jamais vécu!'.[65] It was a way of taking up the challenge thrown down to historians by a novelist like Balzac.[66] The mixture of imaginary biography and *documents authentiques* made it possible to leap at a single bound over a threefold obstacle: the lack of evidence; the lack of importance of the subject (peasants, witches) according to commonly accepted criteria; and the absence of stylistic models. Something of the sort had occurred at the advent of Christianity, when the emergence of new human types – bishops, saints – had prompted the adaptation of the old models of biography and the invention of new ones.[67]

Virginia Woolf's *Orlando* (1928) can be considered an experiment in a converging, though not analogous, direction, since here invention prevails over historiographical reconstruction. Here, the protagonist who proudly traverses the centuries is as marginal a creature as can be imagined: a hermaphrodite. This shows that the narrative procedure I have described is of more than merely technical interest – it is a conscious effort to suggest the existence of historical dimensions that are hidden, in part (but not only) owing to the difficulties of documentary access. A multitude of lives that have been cancelled, destined to count for nothing, find their symbolic redemption in the depiction of immortal characters.[68]

Some might object that none of the examples mentioned thus far can be considered typical of historiographical investigation: even *La Sorcière* (nowadays considered by many to be one of the masterpieces of nineteenth-century historiography) was considered, when it was first published – in a culture already steeped in positivism – as a sort of novel.[69] Let us, then, take a step towards more recent and less controversial history books.

Eileen Power developed with Sir John Chapham the plan for the first edition of the *Cambridge Economic History of Europe*; for many years, right up to her premature death (1941), she taught economic history at the London School of Economics.[70] In 1924 she published *Medieval People*: a book that is still eminently vivid, based on profound research though aimed at an ordinary readership, in which medieval society is presented through a series of portraits of 'quite ordinary people and unknown to fame, with the exception of Marco Polo'. In her preface, the author observes that 'there is often as much material for reconstructing the life of some quite ordinary person as there is for writing a history of Robert of Normandy or of Philippa of Hainault'.[71] This is a provocative idea, and perhaps just a little exaggerated – despite her talent in combining erudition and imagination, Power does not wholly succeed in proving her thesis. It is significant that the two women in the series, Madame Eglentyne and the Ménagier's Wife, are taken from literary texts – each quite different – written by men: Chaucer and the *Ménagier de Paris*, the unidentified author of a book of instructions for his wife, written between 1392 and 1394. Even more significant is the fact that the protagonist of the first chapter of the book, Bodo the peasant, should actually be little more than a name entered in the estate book drawn up during the reign of Charlemagne by Irminon, Abbot of St Germain des Prés. We know that Bodo had a wife, Ermentrude, and three children called Wido, Gerbert, and Hildegard;

we have some information about the land he worked. How can these bare statistics be fleshed out? Power describes the setting in which Bodo worked: she explains the organization of labour in the lands of the abbey; the relationships between the seignorial manse and the little dependent manses; the obligations incumbent upon the peasants; she attempts to 'imagine a day in his life. On a fine spring morning towards the end of Charlemagne's reign Bodo gets up early. . . .' But Power does not stop there: she also attempts to reconstruct Bodo's beliefs, his superstitions: 'If you had followed behind Bodo when he broke his first furrow you would have probably seen him take out of his jerkin a little cake, baked for him by Ermentrude out of different kinds of meal, and you would have seen him stoop and lay it under the furrow and sing: "Earth, Earth, Earth! O Earth, our mother! . . ."' (followed by the text of an Anglo-Saxon incantation).[72]

The differences between the life of Jacques Bonhomme, described with a few details by Augustin Thierry in 1820, and the life of Bodo, depicted minutely by Eileen Power a century later, leap to the eye: in the former, documentary evidence is set forth along the course of twenty centuries, arrayed around a symbolic character; in the latter, in a context given unity of time, around a character who actually existed. In both cases, the same principle is at work: the filling in of documentary gaps, due to a lack of documentation, with the use of elements taken from the larger context (diachronic in the former case, synchronic in the latter). But Power, too, who sets out with realistic, not symbolic, intent, uses that context with considerable elasticity. It really is quite unlikely that Bodo, who lived just outside Paris, would have sung the words of an

Anglo-Saxon incantation. When we read that 'Bodo would certainly take a holiday and go to the fair', we understand immediately that this is a conjecture. But in the face of a phrase that technically makes no conjecture, such as 'Bodo goes whistling off in the cold', it would be naive to wonder whether it is based on a source.[73] The first integration is suggested, like others that recur in the same text, by a judgement of historical compatibility; the second, by a generic consideration of plausibility (peasants whistle today; certainly they whistled during the reign of Charlemagne) that is certainly open to question (men aren't nightingales; whistling is not a natural act).

In the preface to *Medieval People*, Power says that 'social history lends itself particularly to what may be called a personal treatment'. This term should not deceive us – person here is synonymous with 'type', though not with 'ideal type' in the sense suggested by Max Weber.[74] Can someone, however, who is investigating the history of subordinate social groups expect to reconstruct individuals in the fullest sense of the term? Almost thirty years ago, François Furet gave a very clear answer to this question: the lower classes of the past can be studied only in terms of 'number and anonymity, through historical demographics and sociology'.[75] Today, this statement appears quite rigid, if not actually pessimistic. It has been shown, primarily by virtue of judicial sources, that qualitative analyses are possible, working both on court records and, where necessary, with literary elaborations of those records. Natalie Zemon Davis moved in this latter direction in her book *The Return of Martin Guerre*: a case of impersonation and mistaken identity that occurred in a French village in the sixteenth century. This episode gave rise to a remarkable trial, the records of which have been lost, but which is indirectly accessible because of the detailed accounts published by the judge who handed down the verdict, Jean Coras. This documentary situation conditioned Davis's research strategy:

> In the absence of the full testimony from the trial (all such records for criminal cases before 1600 are missing for the Parlement of Toulouse), I have worked through the registers of Parlementary sentences to find out more about the affair and about the practice and attitudes of the judges. In pursuit of my rural actors, I have searched through notarial contracts in villages all over the dioceses of Rieux and Lombez. When I could not find my individual man or woman in Hendaye, in Artigat, in Sajas, or in Burgos, then I did my best through other sources from the period and place to discover the world they would have seen and the reactions they might have had.[76]

One is inevitably reminded of Eileen Power, about whom Davis has written with power and clarity.[77] But Davis is far more careful than Power to distinguish between established truths and possibilities, to point out the supplements to the documentation with a conditional form (or a 'perhaps', a 'probably') rather than hiding them behind an indicative mood. One might compare Davis's approach to modern restoration technique, in which the gaps in a painting are not concealed by repainting, but emphasized by canvas.[78] Context, considered as an array of historically determined possibilities, then serves to fill in what documents fail to tell us about an individual. These integrations, however, are possibilities, not necessary consequences; conjectures, not ascertained facts. Anyone who came to a different conclusion would be rejecting the haphazard and unpredictable dimension that forms such an important part (if not all) of an individual life.

Let us return to the trial of Sofri and his fellow defendants. In it, Investigating Magistrate Lombardi and Assistant District Attorney Pomarici behaved as historians rather than as judges, and that is not all – as rather reckless historians. An innocuous disciplinary transgression, apparently. In reality, it was something quite different.

We began these considerations by emphasizing that judges and historians have a certain shared territory: the ascertaining of facts and, therefore, proof. Bit by bit, we have seen a series of divergences come to light, such as the difference between judicial error and errors in scholarship, which in turn leads to the question (not discussed here) of verdicts.[79] Now, even the convergence between the two disciplines in the area of ascertaining facts proves to be only partial. The facts which judges and historians take under examination are different, in part, chiefly because judges and historians have different attitudes concerning the issue of context – or perhaps we should say contexts. To judges, contexts appear (if we leave aside the question of logical proof, to which we shall immediately return) primarily in the form of mitigating elements or circumstances, of a biological or historical nature. On the basis of them, an individual may be found partially or entirely insane, temporarily or constitutionally unable to understand, and so on; or, a series of crimes may be amnestied because they were committed in exceptional circumstances (civil war, prolonged social conflicts such as those which occurred in Italy in autumn 1969, ıd so on). These elements or circumstances serve to modify a ormal situation, mitigating the principle of culpability, according to which 'no act or form of behaviour has the value of an action unless it is the product of a choice, and consequently, cannot be punished, nor prohibited, unless it is intentional, which is to say, committed with awareness and will by a person capable of understanding and exercising free will'.[80] We have seen that the reduction of every event or historical process to this sort of action is typical of what we have called judicial historiography. This, however, is an unsuccessful line of inquiry in terms of scholarship. For the past century or so, the relationship between human actions and contexts (biological contexts, cultural contexts, economic contexts, and so on) constitutes, rather, for the most vital forms of historiography, an open problem – not a postulate defined once and for all, in one sense or another. This explains the 'ambiguous role' biography has assumed in historical research; as Momigliano has written: 'it may be a tool of social research or it may be an escape from social research'.[81]

The paths of judge and historian, which run side by side for a certain distance, eventually and inevitably diverge. If one attempts to reduce the role of the historian to that of a judge, one simplifies and impoverishes historiographical knowledge; but if one attempts to reduce the role of the judge to that of a historian, one contaminates – and irreparably so – the administration of justice. Certainly, Lombardi is right (against Spataro) to formulate 'logical proof' in terms of compatibility, rather than in terms of necessary derivation from a context; both, however, are wrong when they claim to demonstrate – on the basis of contextual circumstances, and in the absence of any external confirmation – that certain individual actions actually took place. This means slipping tacitly (and illicitly) from the plane of mere possibility to the level of asserting a fact; from the conditional to the indicative. This is a logical error, paradoxically based on an abuse of so-called 'logical proof' (which it would be more reasonable to call 'contextual proof'). In comparison with the errors of historians, however, the errors of judges have more immediate and more serious consequences. They can lead to the conviction of innocent people.

X I X

I am absolutely certain, as I have said, of the innocence of Adriano Sofri. Moral certainty, however, does not have the value of proof. That is why I have not spoken at greater length about my beliefs, which are of no interest to anyone. Instead I have tried to show, through an analysis of the documentation adduced during the trial, that the accusations levelled against Adriano Sofri are entirely groundless. It is truly difficult for me to believe that the judges in Milan, as they delivered their verdict, had *absolutely no doubt* concerning the veracity of Marino's accusations. And the existence of a doubt – however small – with regard to those accusations should have led them to issue an acquittal.

The principle 'in dubio pro reo', by which a defendant can be found guilty only if one is absolutely certain of that guilt, is hardly taken for granted. In 1939, an Italian jurist – Fascist and pro-Nazi – rejected that principle out of hand:

> In case of judicial uncertainty, he [the judge] will rely on the principle *in dubio pro re publica*, which replaces – in the totalitarian state – the ancient principle of *in dubio pro reo*. In a case of uncertainty, the source of legal procedure – in German law – becomes the 'healthy feeling of the populace' [*gesundes Volksempfinden*]. For us, the will of the Duce might serve as that source, as we can understand that will from his word, his teaching, his doctrine.[82]

These principles have not prevailed. The *raison d'état*, or higher interest of the state, has no place (or should have no place) in the courtrooms of our nation. The initial verdict handed down by the Milan Court of Assizes is a judicial error that can – and must – be corrected.

NOTES

[1]See 'Spie. Radici di un paradigma indiziario' (1979), now in *Miti emblemi spie*, Turin 1986 (English edition: 'Clues: Roots of an Evidential Paradigm', in *Clues, Myths, and the Historical Method*, Johns Hopkins University Press, Baltimore, MD, 1989), pp. 158–209; Introduction to P. Burke, *Cultura popolare nell'Europa moderna*, Italian translation, Milan 1980, pp. xiv–xv; 'Prove e possibilità' afterword to Natalie Zemon Davis, *Il ritorno di Martin Guerre* (*The Return of Martin Guerre*, Italian translation), Turin 1984, pp. 131–54, especially p. 151, note 7 (English translation: 'Proofs and Possibilities: In the margins of Natalie Zemon Davis's *The Return of Martin Guerre*', *Yearbook of Comparative and General Literature* 37 [1988], pp. 113–27); 'Montrer et citer', *Le Débat* 566 (September–October 1989), pp. 43–54; 'L'inquisitore come antropologo', in *Studi in onore di Armando Saitta dei suoi allievi pisani*, ed. R. Pozzi and A. Prosperi, Pisa 1989, pp. 23–33; 'Just One Witness', in S. Friedlander, ed., *Probing the Limits of Representation: Nazism and the 'Final Solution'*, Harvard University Press, Cambridge, MA 1992, pp. 82–96, 350–55.

[2]P. Calamandrei, 'Il giudice e lo storico', *Rivista di diritto processuale civile* XII (1939), pp. 105–28, which refers back to G. Calogero, *La logica del giudice e il suo controllo in Cassazione*, 1937.

[3]Thus L. Ferrajoli, *Diritto e ragione. Teoria del garantismo penale*, Bari 1989, pp. 119, 771–3.

[4]See Carlo Ginzburg, *Storia notturna. Una decifrazione del sabba*, Turin 1989, p. XIII (English edition: *Ecstasies: Deciphering the Witches'*

Sabbath, Random House, New York 1991). The comparison between the trial that I am discussing and witch trials was suggested in a letter written by Adriano Prosperi and undersigned by various persons (including this author). The letter was sent to various national Italian newspapers: the only ones that published it were *L'Unità* (11 May 1990) and *il manifesto* (17 May 1990).

[5]See J. Tedeschi, 'The Roman Inquisition and Witchcraft', *Revue d'histoire des religions* 200 (1983), pp. 163–88; Tedeschi, Appunti sulla 'Instructio pro formandis processibus in causis strigum, sortilegorum & maleficiorum', *Annuario dell'Istituto Storico Italiano per l'età moderna e contemporanea*, XXXVIII–XXXIX (1985–86), pp. 219–41; P.H. Jobe, 'Inquisitorial Manuscripts in the Biblioteca Apostolica Vaticana: A Preliminary Handlist' in *The Inquisition in Early Modern Europe: Studies on Sources and Methods*, ed. G. Henningsen and J. Tedeschi, Dekalb, IL 1986, pp. 33–53, esp. pp. 44–5; Carlo Ginzburg, *I benandanti. Stregoneria e culti agrari tra Cinquecento e Seicento*, Turin 1966, pp. 135–7. Tedeschi, who has done the most profound research into the subject, denies that the *Instructio* marked a genuine shift in inquisitorial practice ('Appunti', pp. 238 ff.); still, it strikes me as significant that the call for a return to principles, with which the text begins, should be accompanied by the statement that such principles were hardly ever respected.

[6]See A. Momigliano, 'History between Medicine and Rhetoric' in *Ottavo contributo alla storia degli studi classici e del mondo antico*, Rome 1987, pp. 14–25.

[7]See Ginzburg, 'Montrer et citer'.

[8]See A. Momigliano, 'Storia antica e antiquaria', in *Sui fondamenti della storia antica*, Turin 1984, pp. 5–45.

[9]I consulted the second edition of Griffet's work (Liège 1770). A. Johnson (*The Historian and Historical Evidence*, New York 1926, p. 114), who quotes the passage I have mentioned, calls the *Traité* 'the most significant book on method after Mabillon's *De re diplomatica*'. See also Momigliano, *Sui fondamenti*, p. 19; Ginzburg, 'Just One Witness'. On Gibbon, see, first of all, Momigliano's fundamental essays, *Sui fondamenti*, pp. 294–367.

[10]'The history of the world is the world's court of justice.' See K. Löwith, *Meaning in History: The Theological Implications of the Philosophy of History*, 1949. The phrase (as Alberto Gajano informs me) recurs at least three times in Hegel's work. In general, see Reinhart Koselleck, *Futures Past: On the Semantics of Historical Time* (English edition, The MIT Press, Cambridge, MA 1985).

[11]See Lord Acton, *Lectures on Modern History*, London 1960, p. 17: 'History might be lifted above contention, and made an accepted tribunal, and the same, for all.'

[12]L. Ferrajoli wrote perspicaciously about 'judicial historiography' in an article concerning the so-called 7 April Case [*Caso 7 Aprile*] in *il manifesto*, 23–4 February 1983. This case involved a trial held in Padua against Antonio (Toni) Negri and other members of the extreme left-wing group Autonomia Operaia.

[13]I have made good use of *L'Albero della Rivoluzione. Le interpretazioni della Rivoluzione francese*, ed. B. Bongiovanni and L. Guerci, Turin 1989; in particular, the reader is urged to consult the entries 'Alphonse Aulard' and 'Albert Mathiez' (by M. Vovelle), and 'Hippolyte Taine' (by R. Pozzi). By Aulard, see *Taine historien de la Révolution française*, Paris 1907, prefaced by the characteristic declaration (p. vii): 'Je crois donc être sûr, je ne dis pas de paraître impartial, mais d'être impartial.' [I believe, therefore, that I am sure, not of seeming impartial but of being impartial.] Again, with reference to judiciary metaphors, one should see the title of the anthology of essays by various authors, *Eine Jury für Jacques Roux*, in 'Sitzungsberichte der Akademie des Wissenschaften der DDR' (Gesellschaftswissenschaften) Berlin 1981. On an infinitely more vulgar level, one should see, in Italy, the recent trials of the Risorgimento and of the anti-Fascist Resistance.

[14]See Marc Bloch, *The Historian's Craft*, Manchester 1992.

[15]See the observations concerning Mathiez by François Furet, *Dictionnaire critique de la Révolution française*, Paris 1988, entry 'Histoire universitaire de la Révolution', pp. 990–91 (*A Critical Dictionary of the French Revolution*, Belknap, Cambridge, MA 1989). Concerning *La Grande Peur de 1789* (*The Great Fear of 1789: Rural Panic in Revolutionary France*, Schocken, New York 1973), see the introduction by Jacques

Revel to the French reprint issued in 1989. The juxtaposition of the two books is merely symbolic: it does not take into account, for instance, A. Mathiez, *La vie chère et le mouvement social sous la Terreur*, Paris 1927.

[16]Paris 1924 (*The Royal Touch: Sacred Monarchy and Scrofula in England and France*, Routledge & Kegan Paul, London 1973). See also the entry 'Georges Lefebvre' (by L. Guerci) in *L'Albero della Rivoluzione*.

[17]Brecht's phrase, recorded by Walter Benjamin, is 'Don't start from the good old things but from the bad new ones' (Walter Benjamin, *Understanding Brecht*, Verso, London 1998, p. 121). On the echoes of Giovanni Gentile's philosophy in Hayden White's work (note 19, below), see Ginzburg, 'Just One Witness'.

[18]Marcel Mauss felt differently: see 'Rapports réels et pratiques de la psychologie et de la sociologie' (1924) in *Sociologie et anthropologie*, Paris 1960, pp. 281–310, especially p. 287, where he rejects the tendency to separate 'la conscience du groupe de tout son substrat matériel et concret. Dans la société, il y a autre chose que des représentations collectives, si importantes ou si dominantes qu'elles soient' [group consciousness from all its physical, concrete substratum. There are other things in society besides collective representations, however important or dominant such representations may be], and so on.

[19]Among the most representative figures of this climate, see – from differing points of view – Michel de Certeau (in France) and Hayden White (in the United States). See, respectively, *L'écriture de l'histoire*, Paris 1975 (*The Writing of History*, Columbia University Press, New York 1988) and *Metahistory*, Baltimore, MD 1973. On White, see Momigliano, 'La retorica della storia e la storia della retorica: sui tropi di Hayden White', in *Sui fondamenti*, pp. 465–76; Ginzburg, *Montrer et citer*; 'Just One Witness'. On F. Hartog, *Le miroir d'Hérodote*, Paris 1980, see Ginzburg, 'Proofs and Possibilities', pp. 121–2.

[20]On evidence, see Ferrajoli, *Diritto e ragione*, pp. 108 ff.

[21]See Bloch, *The Historian's Craft*.

[22]See Ferrajoli, *Diritto e ragione*, p. 32.

[23]See, for example, the transcripts of the hearings, pp. 22, 48, 173, 183, 205, 235, 640, 660, etc., transcribed alternately, with great

interpretative intelligence (I am referring especially to the skilful use of punctuation) by M. Bernasconi and L. Scalise.

[24]On all this, see Ferrajoli, *Diritto e ragione*, p. 23; Ginzburg, 'L'inquisitore'.

[25]*Informazioni testimoniali*. Refers to police procedure and testimony in protocol for preliminary investigations.

[26]The pages indicated in parentheses refer, here and elsewhere, to the typewritten transcriptions.

[27]On this point, however, see Adriano Sofri, *Memoria*, Palermo 1990, pp. 62–3.

[28]Ibid., pp. 73–7.

[29]*Confrontation*, p. 6 (the second answer, given previously, was entered into the record at the request of lawyer Gentili, defender of Sofri).

[30]See Sofri, *Memoria*, pp. 45–9, 82–3.

[31]Lucien Febvre, 'Leçon d'ouverture au Collège de France, 13 décembre 1933' in *Combats pour l'histoire*, Paris 1992, p. 8.

[32]Annarumma: the name of a policeman killed during a demonstration in Milan on 19 November 1969; the exact circumstances of his death have never been brought to light.

[33]'But you know, there was nothing on Marino, either in our files or elsewhere . . . you see what I'm saying?', Colonel Bonaventura said. (*Trial*, p. 1696)

[34]'In the presence of the undersigned officers of [Polizia Giudiziaria], members of the previously mentioned [Nucleo Operativo] and of the Company of *carabinieri* of Sarzana . . .' is written in the police report. Captain Meo was stationed in Sarzana at that time. The police report is followed by illegible signatures.

[35]Here I follow, almost to the letter, an observation by Adriano Sofri, *Memoria*, p. 142.

[36]I quote from a stenographic transcript (unofficial) of the summation of Prosecuting Attorney Pomarici.

[37]Sofri, *Memoria*, p. 146.

[38]In an account of the trial that appeared in the daily newspaper *Il Giorno* (27 January 1990) we read: 'Concerning this point [Don

Vincenzi's meeting with the individuals who showed identification as *carabinieri*], the lawyer Gaetano Pecorella insisted with more specific questions: Does this mean that Marino was actually watched or guarded much earlier than his surrender to the *carabinieri*?' Strangely enough, I find no trace of these questions posed by lawyer Pecorella in the transcripts of the courtroom hearings.

[39]Not exactly: on the strange affair of the unpaid fine, see Sofri, *Memoria*, pp. 52–8.

[40]The lawyer Maris described, in summer 1988 (as recounted by Franco Bechis in an article in *Il Sabato*, 20–28 August 1988), how Marino, whom he was defending, had confessed to the crimes he had committed to a *carabiniere* in Bocca di Magra 'with whom he had a relationship – how should I put it? – of familiarity, the way things often are in small towns.'

[41]In the same sense, see Manuela Cartosio's comment (*il manifesto*, 22 February 1990).

[42]As was explained repeatedly during the course of the trial, Marino's younger son was named Giorgio, just like Pietrostefani, purely by coincidence: all Pietrostefani's friends call him 'Pietro'.

[43]Statement published in *La Stampa*, 28 January 1990.

[44]The question of method was reiterated in the memoir sent to the judges before they withdrew for deliberations: 'one must beware of conspiracy theories because they cloud the intelligence, and often collapse into facile explanations' (*Memoria*, p. 139).

[45]M. Cortelazzo and U. Cardinale, *Dizionario di parole nuove*, 1964–84, Turin 1986, p. 61, give the following definition of *dietrologia*: 'Critical analysis of events in an effort to detect, behind the apparent causes, true and hidden designs'. The examples that follow, just the same, all have a relatively pejorative tone, beginning with the earliest one (*La Repubblica*, 16 December 1979): 'In order to try to understand, and not to engage in "dietrologia", we have no choice but to examine a number of hypotheses . . .'. See also ' "Dietrologia" (recent empirical science consisting in the search for all sorts of hidden meanings behind every act or word' (*Corriere della Sera*, 6 February 1981); 'Concerning "dietrologia", science of imagination, culture of suspicion, philosophy

of mistrust, technique of the double, triple, quadruple hypothesis, much irony has been heard in recent times' (*La Stampa*, 3 April 1982).

[46]These words – indeed, the entire subchapter (with the exception of the last sentence) – were written in August–September 1990. Concerning the search conducted in the so-called 'lair' of the Red Brigades in the Via Montenevoso, I had recently read an article in *L'Espresso* (7 August 1988) in which the journalist Franco Giustolisi summarized a conversation which took place between the magistrates Ferdinando Pomarici and Armando Spataro (mentioned frequently in these pages) and the Communist senator Sergio Flamigni, formerly a member of the Moro Commission (on the kidnap and murder of Aldo Moro, and the slaughter of his bodyguards). The article ended with this exchange: '*Flamigni*: "At any rate, Dottor Pomarici, did you really search the apartment in the Via Montenevoso thoroughly?" *Pomarici*: "Stripped bare. Wall by wall. Brick by brick." *Flamigni*: "Yet I will have to have the satisfaction one day of going into the apartment in the Via Montenevoso. Just to see if . . ."' At the beginning of October 1990, during renovation work being done on the apartment in the Via Montenevoso, a cache was discovered, concealed by a simple panel: inside were weapons, money, and 418 pages (photocopied) containing a series of letters, unknown until then, written by Aldo Moro during his captivity. Judge Pomarici, who had 'stripped bare' the apartment twelve years before, explained that during his search the cache and its contents had unfortunately eluded him. Shortly thereafter (17 October), Giulio Andreotti, then Prime Minister of Italy, announced that from 1956 on, a secret military structure (the so-called 'Operazione Gladio') had been operating in Italy, with ties to the American intelligence agencies, and explicit anti-Communist objectives.

[47]See Ginzburg, *Ecstasies*, pp. 12–13, 33–62.

[48]See, for instance, A. Ventura, 'Il problema storico del terrorismo italiano' *Rivista storica italiana* 92 (1980), pp. 125–51; on an intellectual level, I agree only with its emphasis on the importance of the concept of conspiracy.

[49]See Sofri, *Memoria*, pp. 139–52.

[50]I take this information from a memoir by Gaetano Pecorella,

lawyer for the defence of Ovidio Bompressi. It was reported in the
newspaper *Il Giorno* (6 April 1990) in a short article entitled 'Senza
giacca, nessuna certezza'. As for the destruction of evidence, Ferrajoli
insisted on the importance of that issue in a very clear and intelligent
interview, which I read when this book – with the exception of the
Postscript – was already finished: see 'La prova diabolica', *Politica e
Economia*, July–August 1990, pp. 9–11.

[51]In a passage (that any paraphrase would spoil) taken from the
summation by lawyer Maris, counsel to Marino, instead of the Republican lawyer we now find Marino's mother:

> It is more than fear that pushes Marino towards the *carabinieri*
> barracks. There are deeper roots. As a boy, Marino was in a
> boarding school run by Salesian priests; he comes from a Catholic
> family. He was accustomed to answer his mother, who would ask
> him whether he had sinned in deed or evil thought. He went to
> confession, during his childhood and adolescence. And when I
> say that behind his experiences there are two thousand years of
> Holy Communion, I am not using a saccharine, literary
> expression: when you want to free yourself from a weight on your
> shoulders, you go to the priest. And in fact, he goes to his parish
> priest. But, since he was a Fiat factory worker, he also faces the
> responsibility that derives from his secular conscience. And he
> goes to see Senator Bertone, because he is a member of the Italian
> Communist Party, and he wants a sincere relationship with his
> political party. And Bertone tells him: 'Go and turn yourself
> in . . .' (*La Repubblica*, 10 April 1990)

[52]'. . . in my first recorded interrogation', Marino explained in
court (11 January 1990; *Trial*, p. 157), 'I said that it was during a
summer month; evidently, my recollections concerning this episode
were rather vague at that time.'

[53]We might mention a similar factual drift, though in an entirely
different context. Marino said during the preliminary inquest that
after the killing, he took a nonexistent train for Turin at 9.40; during
the trial he corrected himself and spoke of 'a train that left Milan

more or less around 10 a.m., just a few minutes before or just a few minutes after'; in actuality, as the presiding judge pointed out to him, it was much more straightforward than that: a train that left at ten o'clock sharp (*Trial*, pp. 100–101). For other recurring commonplaces in Marino's confessions, see Sofri, *Memoria*, pp. 151–2.

[54]This is what Marino said at the preliminary inquest (p. 12). When lawyer Pecorella mentioned this statement during the trial, implicitly pointing out its improbability, Marino had an outburst of impatience: see Chapter XII above (and *Trial*, p. 234).

[55]See Ginzburg, 'Stregoneria e pietà popolare: note a proposito di un processo modenese del 1519' in *Miti emblemi spie*, pp. 3–28; *I benandanti*.

[56]See Sofri, *Memoria*, pp. 50 ff.

[57]'Reliance upon so-called logical proof is exceedingly dangerous; to venture on to this terrain is like walking into a minefield,' wrote Giandomenico Pisapia and Massimo Dinoia ('Processo Marino' from the 'Note di udienza nell'interesse di Giorgio Pietrostefani' addressed to the section of the Milan Court of Assizes, Rome, June 1990, p. 20).

[58]In his response to Sofri's essay, which was also published in *Società Civile*, Assistant District Attorney Spataro makes no reference to his error on this point.

[59]'We are forbidden to use the word "emergency". . . . It is also forbidden to have any convictions, because they are "theorems". It is also, however, forbidden to have any doubts, because those are "suspicions"; and the culture of suspicion is bad – better for the populace to be obedient and gullible. The concept of "logical proof" is forbidden; to say that two plus two equals four is nothing more than a sociological analysis. Falcone's preliminary inquest is also a sociological analysis, "without a shred of evidence". And then it is forbidden to demand justice, since that demonstrates a thirst for vengeance. And so one step leads to the next.' (N. Dalla Chiesa, *Storie di boss ministri tribunali giornali intellettuali cittadini*, Turin 1990, pp. 93–4).

[60]See above, Chapter 11.

[61]See A. Momigliano, *The Development of Greek Biography*, Harvard University Press, Cambridge, MA 1993, pp. 2–3.

[62]Ibid., pp. 12–14, 38–42.

[63]This translation of Hegel's term is taken from A. J. Ayer and Jane O'Grady, *A Dictionary of Philosophical Quotations*, Blackwell Reference, Oxford/Cambridge, MA 1992. (*Translator's note*)

[64]Thierry's short essay first appeared in *Censeur Européen* (12 May 1820); see R. Pozzi's introduction to A. Thierry, *Scritti Storici*, Turin 1983, p. 26, which in general underscores the importance of the young Thierry's collaboration with Saint-Simon. The essay was then republished in *Dix ans d'études historiques*, Paris 1835; I consulted the Milan [=Paris] edition (1843), where it is on pp. 202–8; on p. 207 there is mention of 'plaisanterie'. See L. Gossmann, 'Augustin Thierry and Liberal Historiography' *History and Theory*, Beiheft 15, 1976. See also M. Gauchet, *Les lieux de la mémoire*, II, I, Paris 1986, pp. 247–316. For the English edition of *La Sorcière*, see *Witchcraft, Sorcery, and Superstition*, Carol Publishers, New York 1992.

[65]'Le Crépuscule du Soir', last verses: 'Encore la plupart n'ont-ils jamais connu / La douceur du foyer et n'ont jamais vécu!' [Yet most of them never knew / The pleasures of hearth and home, and never truly lived!] (Charles Baudelaire, *Les Fleurs du Mal*, in *Œuvres complètes*, ed. Y.-G. Le Dantec, Paris 1954, p. 167).

[66]See Ginzburg, 'Proofs and Possibilities'.

[67]See A. Momigliano, 'Marcel Mauss e il problema della persona nella biografia greca', in *Ottavo contributo*, pp. 179–90; and 'The Life of St Macrina by Gregory of Nyssa', ibid., pp. 333–47.

[68]The central idea of *Orlando* may derive from *She, a History of Adventure*, a novel by Henry Rider Haggard, published in 1887 and often reprinted.

[69]See P. Viallaneix, preface to J. Michelet, *La Sorcière*, Paris 1966, p. 20.

[70]See M. M. Postan, preface to the *Storia Economica Cambridge*, III, Italian edition of the *Cambridge Economic History of Europe*, Turin 1977. On Eileen Power, seen in parallel with Bloch, see Natalie Zemon Davis, 'History's Two Bodies', *American Historical Review* 93 (1988), pp. 1–30, especially pp. 18 ff.

[71]See Eileen Power, *Medieval People*, New York/Evanston, IL/San Francisco/London 1963 (1st edn 1924), p. ix.

[72]Ibid., p. 28 (and see the entire chapter, pp. 18–38).

[73]See ibid. Note that in the previous phrase, 'certainly' means 'quite probably' (this is a common habit among historians; I do not know if the same is true of judges).

[74]See Zemon Davis, 'History's Two Bodies', p. 22, which also refers to Eileen Power, 'On Medieval History as a Social Study', *Economica*, n.s. 1 (1934), pp. 13–29, especially pp. 20–21 (where she criticizes Max Weber).

[75]See François Furet, 'Pour une définition des classes inférieures à l'époque moderne', *Annales ESC* XVIII (1963), pp. 459–74, especially p. 459 (quoted by Carlo Ginzburg in *Il Formaggio e i vermi*, Turin 1976, p. xix; English edition, *The Cheese and the Worms*, Baltimore, MD 1980, p. xx).

[76]See Natalie Zemon Davis, *The Return of Martin Guerre*, Harvard University Press, Cambridge, MA, 1983, pp. 6–7.

[77]See Zemon Davis, 'History's Two Bodies'.

[78]See Ginzburg, 'Proofs and Possibilities', especially pp. 116, 120–21.

[79]Calamandrei is particularly insistent on this point in his essay 'Il giudice e lo storico'. He recognizes the validity of the thesis set forth by Croce in *Filosofia della Pratica*, according to which judicial activity, comparable to the phase of ascertaining the facts in historiography, becomes, in its final phase (the verdict), comparable to the act of will, a political act. Calamandrei observes that this thesis, which he considers valid in purely theoretical terms, might have exceedingly dangerous practical consequences in a situation where – in emulation of the model of Soviet Russia and Nazi Germany – there was widespread support in Italy for judges 'expressing a political will that arises and is affirmed with the verdict' (the reference is to positions similar to that expressed at the same time by G. Maggiore, in his essay 'Diritto penale totalitario nello stato totalitario', cited in Note 82 below). Calamandrei concludes with a proposal that the judge 'should continue to consider himself nothing more than a modest and faithful

historian of law, and to behave as such', committing 'a philosophical error, but an innocuous error in practical terms, which will do nothing to harm justice' (p. 125). A discussion of the avowed theoretical weakness of this compromise solution is of no interest in this context.

[80]See Ferrajoli, *Diritto e ragione*, p. 491.

[81]See Momigliano, *The Development of Greek Biography*, p. 8; quoted by G. Levi, 'Les usages de la biographie', *Annales ESC* 44 (1989), pp. 1325–6, which should be consulted for an intelligent treatment on the present-day meaning of these terms.

[82]See G. Maggiore, 'Diritto penale totalitario nello stato totalitario', *Rivista italiana di diritto penale* XI (1939), p. 159.

POSTSCRIPT

The written judgement of the verdict against Adriano Sofri and his fellow defendants has finally been published. The judgement comprises 753 pages (plus indices), explaining – with a wealth of detail – the reasons that led the Milan Court of Assizes to issue the heavy sentences mentioned above.

A technical analysis of this document is, of course, beyond my abilities. What interests me here, once again, are the divergences and convergences between judge and historian. About the divergences I really need not say any more. As for the convergences, let me do no more than note that the questions that arose in my mind as I read the transcripts and records of the trial focused primarily on matters (evidence, circumstances) that had to be taken into account by the assistant judge who drew up the written judgement and the presiding judge who countersigned it. In order to facilitate a comparison between their work and my own, I have chosen to draw a clear distinction between the two phases of research and writing that went into this book. In this way, the reader can clearly see the processes that led me and the judges to such widely differing – indeed, opposite – conclusions.

(*a*) *The carabinieri.* The interpretation of the trial that I set forth emphasized in particular the courtroom testimony of the *carabinieri*, and the ensuing attempt to backdate their relationship with Marino. On this point, the judgement declares:

> It is rare that a trial is held in which the source of proof is testimony of complicity on the part of a defendant without suspicion being cast upon the *carabinieri* or the police or upon some magistrate, with insinuations that they may have exerted pressure of some sort or offered benefits or rewards to unscrupulous prisoners, or that they may have 'personalized' their relations with state's witnesses.
>
> In the case in question, not only was Marino not a prisoner, a defendant, or a suspect – so that it is hard to say what pressure might have been employed to 'force' him to claim responsibility for a murder and other criminal acts – but it was the *carabinieri* themselves, summoned to testify on the initiative of this court, who contradicted the witness and introduced a new element undermining his credibility, so that if the defence wishes to speculate concerning illicit judicial behaviour or behaviour that might undermine the credibility of the defendant and witness for the prosecution, there can be no doubt that in this specific case the hypothesis of collusion between the *carabinieri* and the said defendant/prosecution witness is clearly groundless. (*Judgement*, pp. 215–16)

As the reader can see, the judgement fails to note that the *carabinieri* waited nearly two years before contradicting the defendant/prosecution witness (i.e. Marino), as well as the fact that they were not summoned to testify until the testimony of another witness (Don Regolo Vincenzi) demolished the official version of Marino's repentance and confession. To argue concerning this matter while overlooking these two fundamental points (upon which see above, Chapters X ff.) appears to me to be arguing in a way that is 'clearly groundless' – in the sense that one leaves standing all the inconsistencies that one claims to be trying to resolve.

(*b*) *The circumstances and the evidence: the robberies*. In Chapter XVII, I attempted to parse, on the basis of the statements made after the conclusion of the trial by Assistant District Attorney Armando Spataro, the reasoning that led to the guilty verdict. I reconstructed it as follows:

> . . . if (1) the robberies that Marino claims to have taken part in are proven; if (2) some of them were committed, according to Marino, on behalf of the so-called illegal group within Lotta Continua; then (3) Marino's confessions concerning the order to kill Calabresi issued by the so-called executive committee and (4) concerning the role played in instigating this killing by Pietrostefani and Sofri may be accepted without any objective corroboration.

The written judgement demonstrates that my conjectural reconstruction was accurate. I will not bother to repeat the reasons that lead me to judge this analysis – which offers up a set of circumstances, real or claimed, in lieu of proof of specific criminal acts – to be entirely unacceptable (see above, Chapters

XVII and XVIII). The court has adopted it; but with some inconsistencies.

Let us begin with the robberies. In this context, not all Marino's accusations were accepted. Mottura, Bompressi and Pedrazzini, for instance – who, Marino claimed, took part in a bank robbery in Saluggia (Mottura) and another robbery of the Nuovo Pignone in Massa (Bompressi and Pedrazzini) – were all acquitted as innocent. The written judgement of the verdict states, with reference to Bompressi and Pedrazzini:

> . . . it should be noted that the further elements supporting Marino's declarations should be considered not solely in relation to the individual defendants (when the defendant/witness indicates Bompressi and Pedrazzini, he mentions a person roughly 1.8 metres in height, with chestnut hair, and another person wearing glasses) but also in relation to the individual episode (robbery at Saluggia: Marino states that, besides the 'Venetian', Bompressi, Pedrazzini, and Sibona entered the bank, and the witnesses described a person about 1.8 metres tall and a person wearing glasses).
>
> The fact, then, that there is no element in the robbery at Nuovo Pignone indicating the presence of Bompressi and Pedrazzini – consequently, the decision has been made to acquit them, since it is impossible to rule out errors – does not undermine Marino's reliability in any way, both because Bompressi did not physically take part in the robbery, and because the victims of the robbery were immobilized, by a sudden ambush, inside their car at gunpoint, and in fact both the victims and the witness Pucciarelli,

overtaken while the robbers were making their escape, failed to give more than a sketchy description of a few of the robbers. (*Judgement*, pp. 746–7)

This reasoning, which might seem at first sight to be the product of a scrupulous zeal for equitable procedure, actually betrays quite the opposite – specifically that in the search for objective verification of Marino's accusations, decidedly broad strokes were accepted. After all, a robber about 1.8 metres tall or a robber wearing glasses are not such rare occurrences that they can provide incontrovertible identification. (I must admit that I may have a vested interest in making the above statement, since I am about 1.8 metres tall and I often wear glasses.) For Sibona and Gracis, on the other hand, who were also accused by Marino of having taken part in the robbery of the Nuovo Pignone – though the statute of limitations had already expired with the application of the mitigating circumstances allowed by Italian law – there was not even this (insignificant) level of corroborative evidence.

Concerning Sibona, the judgement states:

. . . possible errors in the identification of this defendant as a participant in the robbery of the bank in Saluggia and the robbery at the 'Nuovo Pignone' plant are excluded, respectively, by the episode of the child who knocked at the door of the bank during the robbery and by the 'Di Calogero episode' [Di Calogero was involved, according to Marino, in the attempt to 'kneecap' a right-wing leader]; these are specific episodes whose intrinsic content is such that we can reasonably rule out the idea that the defendant/ witness might have erroneously linked Sibona with those acts. (*Judgement*, pp. 742–3)

There is no need for objective corroboration: Marino proves the truth of Marino's words. Marino, at least in these two cases, cannot be wrong (the possibility that he is lying is not even taken into consideration).

And Gracis? Gracis

... has denied all accusations, and claims that in the sum- mer of 1971 – immediately after the meeting in Bologna – he went to Spain with friends, until the end of August. Actually, Marino also makes reference to that holiday, but states that Gracis went on holiday to Spain only after the robbery; and it is actually safe to consider this as evidence against the defendant, since on the one hand there is no evidence that the defendant left at the end of July, and on the other it is not clear how Marino managed to learn of Gracis's holiday. (*Judgement*, pp. 744–5)

Overwhelming proof, as we can see. It does not take much imagination to see that Marino might have learned of Gracis's holiday from anyone (from Gracis himself, for instance). Is the fact that Gracis actually did go to Spain on holiday (we do not know when) sufficient evidence that Marino is telling the truth when he describes him as a robber? Unquestionably, Marino did take part in some of the robberies he describes. But – with- out objective corroboration – how can we say that he has not accused innocent people?

(c) The circumstances and the evidence: the meeting of the executive committee. The foregoing shows that in the chain of reasoning adopted by the court, the robberies described by Marino – meant to show the existence of an illegal group within Lotta Continua – are a weak link. Another link is even less substantial – indeed, it is ectoplasmic: the decision to assassinate Calabresi, made by the executive committee of Lotta Continua. Marino – once again the sole source – specified during the preliminary inquest that the decision was ordered by a majority vote, and he went so far as to give the names of those in favour and those against. Among those against, Marco Boato (who was not, for that matter, even a member of the executive committee) immediately and indignantly denied this insinuation, and demanded that he be formally accused in order to have an opportunity to prove his innocence. His request was ignored. Both Boato and Viale, another member of the executive committee who (according to Marino's account) supposedly voted against killing Calabresi, testified at length in court. The presiding judge questioned neither of them about the supposed meeting of the executive. It seemed reasonable to infer from this fact that Marino was considered unreliable on this point, which was clearly crucial. As we read the written judgement, however, we find that the meeting of the executive committee was adopted to solve a difficulty raised (*nota bene*) by the presiding judge himself during the trial.

I have already examined this point at some length (Chapter V above). Marino had admitted that someone called him in Turin to alert him that everything was ready for the assassination. It was not clear whether, following his talk with Sofri in Pisa, Marino had ever notified the others of his willingness to take part. Let us reread the exchange between Presiding Judge Minale and Marino, which took place during the session of 15 January:

Presiding judge: 'In effect, the organizer was still not certain that you would be taking part, and in fact Pietrostefani said to you, "You, Marino, still have some doubts. If you still have doubts, go to Pisa." You went to Pisa and you resolved your doubts. But – and this is the point – did you inform Pietrostefani that you had resolved your doubts?'

Marino: 'No.'

Presiding judge: 'You didn't see Pietrostefani again?'

Marino: 'No.'

Presiding judge: 'Between the 13th and the 17th . . .'

Marino: 'I saw him again . . . no, no . . . I saw him again later . . .'

Presiding judge: 'Nor did you see Enrico [= Bompressi]?'

Marino: 'No.'

Presiding judge: 'Then, Enrico had already left on his own?'

Marino: 'Yes, I saw him again in Milan . . .'

Presiding judge: 'What I mean to say is, then, that the go-ahead had been given for the operation, even before you had fully agreed to participate?'

[*Stenographer's note: Marino does not answer the presiding judge's question.*]

Presiding judge: 'Well then, you don't know!'

Marino: 'I don't know.'

Presiding judge: 'The simple fact is that Enrico had already left prior to the 13th, and then you told Pietrostefani nothing at all about the fact that you were now willing to participate?'

Marino: 'No.' (*Trial*, pp. 281–2)

Marino's confusion in the face of the presiding judge's questioning is evident. During the course of the trial, however, as I have tried to show above (Chapters VI ff.), the presiding judge changed his mind. Evidently, exchanges like the one I have just quoted persuaded him (for reasons that elude me) of Marino's credibility. We have further evidence of this change of heart in a passage from the written judgement of the verdict, which the presiding judge countersigned, along with its author, Assistant Judge Proietto. Here Marino is rescued from the quicksand into which the presiding judge himself had cast him.

> When, following the death of Serantini, Pietrostefani had informed him that it was necessary to move more quickly in the wake of that event, the fact that the date had been established is a circumstance that in no way clashes with Marino's account, because the decision had come down from the executive committee, and Pietrostefani knew perfectly well that Sofri was in agreement and therefore he was certain that Marino would participate, because Sofri could not have failed to confirm to Marino what Pietrostefani had already told Marino: that the decision originated with the organization in question, and that Sofri was in agreement.
>
> Thus, on the one hand, in Pisa the subject of discussion was considerably narrowed and, on the other, once this confirmation had been given, there was not much left to

talk about, nor did Pietrostefani need to know whether Marino had agreed to participate or not, because he was perfectly aware of what the outcome of that discussion would be. (*Judgement*, pp. 516–17)

It is not clear how this 'perfect awareness' on Pietrostefani's part fits with the doubts, the reluctance, and the concerns that Marino had expressed (by his own account) in his conversation with Sofri in Pisa:

Sofri said that he had the greatest confidence in Enrico [= Bompressi] and myself, and he further reassured me, telling me that if by some chance I were caught or killed, provision would be made for my family, and especially for my son. My misgivings about the operation were based in part on the fact that I had a young son, and I was worried about him, about what would happen to him if I were killed or arrested. He offered sweeping reassurances . . . (*Preliminary Inquest*, p. 13; see above, Chapter V)

There is, however, a more substantial problem. The reasoning set forth in the written judgement is dependent upon an event whose existence is demonstrated, as has been noted, solely by Marino's testimony: the meeting at which the executive committee of Lotta Continua supposedly decided, by a majority vote, to have Calabresi assassinated. On this point, towards the end of the written judgement, we read:

Marino states, saying that he learned this from Bompressi, Pietrostefani, and Sofri, that the decision [to kill Calabresi] came from the national executive committee; likewise the information that not all the members were in agreement was second-hand.

Who physically took part in that decision is not given to us to know, though it certainly seems unlikely that so weighty a responsibility would have been taken on by Sofri and Pietrostefani alone, and that it would have been shared among the leadership (whether or not that coincided with the entire membership of that body, and whether they decided unanimously or not), although they were indeed the most important members of that organization: Sofri claims to be the founder and leader of the movement . . . and concerning Pietrostefani he states that he was 'a well-known and important figure in LC', and the latter [Pietrostefani] has stated that he was a national leader of the movement.

Now, if the killing can be attributed to Lotta Continua for the reason indicated above, if we can rule out the hypothesis that the killing was an isolated act on the part of Marino and the other person who materially committed the murder, or of both of them as members of some internal faction of the movement, if the killing could have been ordered only by the executive body of Lotta Continua – which revolved around Sofri and Pietrostefani, whether formally or otherwise – and if within the movement there existed an illegal group created by the decision of that executive body, and especially Sofri and Pietrostefani, in order to finance the movement, and if a member of that group took part in killing, all of this, in the view of the court, constitutes an objective corroboration to the accusation by the defendant/witness of Sofri and Pietrostefani. (*Judgement*, pp. 705–7)

'If ..., if ..., if. ...' In this reasoning, everything is eva-
nescent, beginning with the famous meeting of the executive
committee; impossible to verify because reported only through
second-hand knowledge, but necessary in order to involve
Lotta Continua (in the persons of two of its most prestigious
leaders) in the planning and implementation of the murder of
Calabresi. Marino (according to the written judgement) did not
need to inform Pietrostefani of his conversation with Sofri,
because after the meeting of the executive committee Pietrostefani already knew that Sofri was in agreement; but the
source of the executive committee meeting, of the conversation
in Pisa between Marino and Sofri, of the previous conversations between Pietrostefani and Marino, is always and only
one: Marino. How can we even talk about 'objective corroboration' in this context? There is no corroboration: there is only
the word of Marino. But is Marino reliable?

(*d*) *Marino's reliability.* Clearly, this question lies at the foundation of the entire trial. The court, as we know, answered it
in the affirmative. The written judgement tells us the terms in
which the question was put:

> It is necessary ... to examine whether, in the evaluation
> of credibility, the other elements of proof must confirm the
> statements on every individual point, or whether, rather, it
> is sufficient that those elements confirm the statements of
> the co-defendant on the whole. ... It is not possible to

establish a rule that is valid always and in every case, and it is necessary to judge from case to case, taking into account specific aspects of the concrete case.

In the evaluation of statements concerning a few facts, which can be easily circumscribed, for example, the elements offered to the judge for his judgement of reliability are generally limited, and in such cases the divisibility of statements is preferable, so that one may consider as proven only those facts that can be objectively corroborated, so as to avoid operations of transferred credibility.

Where, on the other hand, the statements concern numerous acts and involve a great number of individuals, encompassing vast areas, the absence of an element of proof (because it is impossible to acquire that evidence, because a great deal of time has passed, because of shortcomings on the part of the investigating authorities, or for other reasons) that serves to corroborate an episode, or links a person to a certain act, may not result in the divisibility of the statements mentioned above, if – considering the personality of the co-defendant/witness, of the probative value of the other elements of evidence acquired, their nature and their quantity – the latter have integrated the imperfect evidentiary capacity of the said element of proof . . .

In the concrete case, moreover, and as we shall see, where the crime of homicide is concerned, there are specific elements of evidence that confirm the reliability of the accuser on both the act and the persons accused as accomplices.

As far as other criminal episodes are concerned, it has

been determined that the overall reliability of the accuser's statements also proves the participation of several defendants in the activity of the illegal group. (*Judgement*, pp. 198–9, 201)

The court, then, in evaluating Marino's statements, has admitted the legitimacy of 'operations of transferred credibility' concerning the robberies ('the other criminal episodes'), by stating that concerning the murder, specific corroborative evidence had been obtained instead. These are worrisome statements. As the reader has seen: (1) Marino's presumed 'overall reliability' concerning the robberies does not exclude the possibility of his inaccuracies or lies concerning specific events; (2) the robberies carried a decisive burden in the argument that led to the conviction of Sofri, Pietrostefani and Bompressi. The written judgement itself thus recognizes that an unspecified portion of the case for the prosecution rests upon 'operations of transfer of credibility' (or contagion of credibility); if Marino told the truth about points a, b and c, then he can also be considered reliable upon points x, y and z. But a, b and c might be unimportant circumstances, of no significance to the purposes of the trial: their relationship to points x, y and z might be aleatory (see above, Chapters XVII and XVIII). And in that case?

As far as the murder is concerned, however – the written judgement reassures us – 'there are specific elements of evidence that confirm the reliability of the defendant/accuser' that is to say, Marino.

As the reader will no doubt recall, in examining the divergences (and in some cases these are head-on contradictions) between Marino's version and the testimony of eyewitnesses to the murder, I had concluded (see above, especially Chapter XV) that, in all likelihood, Marino is lying about the murder. The written judgement explores, point by point, the same divergences, and comes to the opposite conclusion. Let me check the soundness of that conclusion, beginning with the exceedingly minute and intricate discussion (*Judgement*, pp. 238–9) of the collision involving Giuseppe Musicco not far from the killing, just a few minutes before it occurred.

(*e*) *Marino's reliability: the witness Musicco*. Let me reproduce here, for clarity's sake, the versions of the accident provided by Marino and by Musicco (see also above, Chapter XV, sub-chapter *a*).

Marino (10 January 1990; *Trial*, p. 103; and see previously, *Preliminary Inquest, Police Report*, p. 12):

> As I was driving out of the parking lot, I had in fact this small collision[*a fender-bender – Author's note*] with another car which, evidently, was looking for a parking place (was driving into the parking lot). The accident scared me a bit, because I was driving a stolen car, and I certainly could not show this gentleman the registration of the automobile or stop to argue, and so, with a glance, I indicated to him ... (I made a gesture with one hand, for this gentleman to reverse slightly, so as to clear the way, as it were, and indicating to him that I would stop immediately afterwards to give him my documents or whatever). This gentleman reversed for a short distance, and I, in fact, as soon as the way was clear, took off suddenly, towards the exit of the

parking lot (in practical terms, the road away from the parking lot).

Musicco (31 January 1990; *Trial*, pp. 921 ff.):

'I was parked,' he had said, 'in my car near the subway entrance; but then, as I was driving out of the parking lot, at the intersection a car went by at high speed; it smashed into me and knocked me around and I didn't see a thing; I stopped and didn't see another thing.'

As the reader can see, the two versions cannot be reconciled. Musicco says that he was hit *as he was driving out of* the parking lot, in the direction of the Via Cherubini; while Marino says that he hit this unidentified gentleman *as he was entering* the same parking lot. Musicco says he was hit by a car that took off without stopping; Marino says he was involved in an exchange of sign language with the unidentified gentleman in order to persuade him to back up, so that he could drive away. How can we resolve these contradictions?

For the court, the witness Musicco is not credible, because:

(1) He states that he went to the COIN department store one hour before the accident [about 9.15 a.m.], and this cannot be so inasmuch as no department store is open at that time.

(2) He states that he was hit by another automobile at the corner of the Via Giotto and the Via Cherubini, but this is totally inconsistent with the points of impact.

(3) He states that the car that hit him was travelling at high speed and caused considerable damage, and this is totally inconsistent with the seriousness of the dents.

(4) He can provide no certain information concerning the col-

our and type of car that hit him, nor concerning the people on board that car, nor whether this car continued towards the Via Cimarosa, or whether it then made a turn (*Judgement*, p. 264).

In reality, the author of the written judgement then seems to go even further, even so far as to question the very existence of the accident:

> And if we look carefully, it is a strange accident, because the only people who mention it, and who learned of it in some manner, are Cislaghi and Mattiolo, who each have a store at no. 3, Via Cherubini, and they speak about it because that is where [Musicco's] Simca was parked following the killing; no witness claims to have seen the accident except Musicco himself, and he doesn't even see that well ('a car went by at high speed, it smashed into me and knocked me around and I didn't see a thing; I stopped and didn't see another thing'). (*Judgement*, pp. 257–8)

The attempt to demolish the credibility of the witness by focusing on his faulty memory and physical defects (Musicco is a complete invalid) is – all ethical questions aside – unpersuasive. To be mistaken about an irrelevant event, which took place eighteen years before (1); to exaggerate the dimension of a crash of which one is a victim (3); to state that one is unable to remember the colour and direction of travel of a car that has just hit one's own car and then driven off 'at high speed' (4) are all perfectly understandable forms of behaviour (let me leave aside point (2) for the moment). In any case, a few pages after the observations quoted above, the authors of the written judgement conclude: 'We can state that [Musicco's] Simca had an accident with the car driven by the killers' (*Judgement*, p. 269).

In his statements following the accident, Musicco *supposed* that the car which hit his was the Fiat 125 driven by the killers. In a memoir by lawyer Pecorella (defence lawyer for Bompressi), this identification was questioned – the dents found on the body of the Fiat 125 abandoned following the assassination might have been the result of an accident involving the same car when it was robbed a number of months earlier. That hypothesis, in turn, suggested another, more unsettling hypothesis: that Marino had described the accident (which never actually took place) at the exit from the parking lot, immediately prior to the assassination, by combining the reports of the accident with the reports on the dents received by the Fiat 125. The written judgement rejects these conjectures, adducing what may be perfectly solid grounds, but grounds which (for a reason that I will explain in the next subchapter) necessarily and admittedly remain incomplete, and not entirely verifiable.

So – the court accepted not only the core of Musicco's version (that he was involved in an accident just minutes before the assassination) but even the conjecture he had formed (the unknown car was driven by the killers). All the same, the written judgement states that 'the testimony of Giuseppe Musicco is unusable for any reconstruction of the accident inasmuch as it is clearly inconsistent with objective findings of the trial' (*Judgement*, p. 269). Immediately after that, the author examines the 'statements' made by Marino in this connection.

The plural ('statements') was in fact indispensable. In the

on-site investigation conducted on 4 March 1990, in fact, Marino substantially modified the version he had first supplied during the preliminary inquest, and then confirmed in court:

> The accident occurred not while I was driving out of the parking lot but inside the parking lot, while I was leaving my parking place in the line of cars and the other car was moving forward inside the parking lot in the space between the first line of parked cars, again parallel with the course of the Via Giotto adjoining the pavement, and the first line inside the parking lot itself; the car was moving forward parallel with the course of the Via Giotto in the direction of the Via Cherubini. (*Judgement*, p. 269)

In court, Marino had stated that, after the accident he drove round the block; then he stopped 'for more than fifteen minutes' with his engine running in front of a fruit-and-vegetable stand, located ten metres from Calabresi's residence (see above, Chapter XV, subchapter *b*). This account has many improbable aspects: among other things, Marino would have exposed himself to considerable risk, in that Musicco, who was just across the road, would have been able to recognize the car that had just hit his. Marino, according to the defence, attempted to eliminate this element of implausibility by moving the accident (and therefore Musicco) from the exterior to the interior of the parking lot. This, of course, is a hypothesis. That Marino, however, provided a different version of the accident during the on-site investigation from the one that he had given previously is not a hypothesis: it is an undeniable fact.

In the written judgement, an effort was made to deny this fact, with what can only be described as remarkable reasoning.

During the preliminary inquest, Marino had made the following statement: 'Before driving the Fiat 125 out of the parking area, I had a minor accident: as I was about to drive out, in fact, perhaps because I was nervous or perhaps slightly distracted, I drove my fender against the fender of another car which was preparing to enter the same parking area in search of a place to park.'

In the written judgement, that passage was interpreted as follows:

> These were Marino's first statements concerning the accident, and they begin with the phrase 'Before driving the Fiat 125 out of the parking area, I had a minor accident': this cannot mean anything other than that what he is about to relate occurred 'in the interior of the parking lot' – nor can one hypothesize that the following phrase, followed as it is by a colon, serves to explain the first phrase, since this punctuation mark was certainly not placed there by Marino.
>
> And in fact he continues by describing the mechanics of the accident and stating: 'as I was about to drive out'; this parenthetical statement, given the preceding statement, cannot refer to anything other than the limited area within the parking lot, the place in which the Fiat 125 had been parked during the night of 15 May. (*Judgement*, pp. 273–4)

A simple fact leads to untenable conclusions. It is evident that the colon was inserted not by Marino but by whoever transcribed the interrogation during the preliminary inquest. Above (in Note 23) I spoke of the 'great interpretative intelligence (I am referring especially to the skilful use of punctuation)' of M. Bernasconi and L. Scalise, who transcribed the courtroom testimony. To transcribe the spoken word properly is a complex operation which requires a good ear and a profound understanding of language. In the case we are examining, the colon indicates a pause – less marked than a full stop – perceived by the stenographer immediately following the phrase 'Before driving the Fiat 125 out of the parking area, I had a minor accident'. Without a pause after the words 'minor accident', the sentence makes no sense. The observation quoted above, however, concerning the colon, makes no sense either. Even if the stenographer had inserted a full stop instead of a colon, the explanatory value of the words that immediately follow ('as I was about to drive out, in fact, perhaps because I was nervous or perhaps slightly distracted, I drove my fender against') would have remained intact. That value is a result of the conjunction 'in fact', an obvious fact that eluded the self-appointed philologist who drew up the written judgement.

The words 'as I was about to drive out, in fact', then, serve to narrow the meaning of the words that precede them ('before driving the Fiat 125 out of the parking area'). As we have seen, the written judgement claims that 'parking area' here means the 'limited area within the parking lot', not the 'parking lot': on that point, then, Marino supposedly never changed his story. This interpretation, however, is untenable, as we can see from the following comparison of the two phrases:

(Marino, during the preliminary inquest): 'Before driving

the Fiat 125 out of the parking area, I had a minor accident: as I was about to drive out, in fact ... I drove my fender against ...'

(Marino, during the on-site investigation): 'The accident occurred not while I was driving out of the parking lot, but inside the parking lot.'

Anyone who has even a rudimentary knowledge of language will understand that the second phrase ('not while I was driving out of the parking lot, but inside the parking lot') explicitly corrects and contradicts the first phrase ('as I was about to drive out [of the parking lot]').

If, however (the written judgement continues), the accident had taken place at the exit of the parking lot that gives on to the Via Giotto, as Musicco claims, the two cars would have had something approximating a head-on crash: instead, the Simca had dents on the front left fender; the Fiat 125, on the front right fender (this is point (2) in the list reproduced above). Therefore, the court finds, Marino (the Marino of the second version) is telling the truth. At this juncture, however, a new complication emerges. The dents on the two cars demonstrate, according to the written judgement, that 'it was the Simca that hit the Fiat 125' – a fact that contradicts both Musicco's ('a car went by at high speed; it smashed into me and knocked me around') and Marino's ('as I was about to drive out, in fact, perhaps because I was nervous or perhaps slightly distracted, I drove my fender against') versions.

'How should we evaluate this contrast?' the written judgement asks. The answer to this question (which, as we shall see, refers to Marino alone) should be given in its entirety, respecting the author's grammar and punctuation:

As far as the first question is concerned – the statement made [by Marino] during the preliminary inquest that he had 'driven with his fender against the other car' – it is the court's opinion that this is an element (determined either by the fact that to him the distinction between driving against or being driven against was entirely secondary – in part because he had no particular reason for paying attention to it – or else from a pure and simple vagueness of expression) that is entirely unfit to undermine the reliability of Marino on this point.

One might observe that this is a strange approach, because when the location of the dents contradicts Musicco, the witness becomes unreliable; but when the same dents contradict Marino, the contradiction becomes an unimportant matter.

In reality, the situations are entirely different.

Musicco, as has been noted, is unreliable *per se*, leaving Marino aside, because of the version he gives of the accident, which is inconsistent not only with the location of the dents, but equally inconsistent with the seriousness and size of those dents (the Simca had supposedly been 'knocked around' by the impact, and had supposedly been 'badly damaged') in relation to the mechanics of the accident (the car that hit Musicco's car was travelling at 'high speed') and for the other reasons previously stated.

Marino, on the other hand, as has just been noted, gives a version that is perfectly consistent with the other findings of the court, in which the element just noted is the only inconsistent feature. (*Judgement*, pp. 278–9)

Just why Musicco should be considered 'unreliable *per se*' is not clear. For sixteen years – that is to say, until Marino appeared on the scene of the investigation of the Calabresi assassination – Musicco had been the sole source concerning the accident we are discussing. From the written judgement it would appear, as we have seen, that the court entirely accepted the conjecture offered by Musicco immediately following the killing: that the other car involved in the accident was the Fiat 125 driven by the killers. And so? One might gather that Musicco is unreliable in the court's view not '*per se*' (a statement that has something almost metaphysical about it) but only when he talks about the site of the accident. Then why should Marino be considered reliable, when he identifies the site of the accident eighteen years later? Marino, who changes his version during the course of an on-site investigation, having offered – first in the preliminary inquest and later in court – a version that fully coincided with Musicco's version concerning this point?

And that is not all. During the course of the on-site investigation, in response to a question from the defence, Marino added a new detail: 'The car came from my right, very slowly, as if it were looking for a place to park. Let me state that had the other car not backed up, I would have been unable to leave the line of parked cars, because there was another parked car behind me.'

In an effort to reconcile this statement with the dents on the two cars, the written judgement breaks up the grim darkness of the judicial proceedings with a few pages of involuntary hilarity:

As far as the second question is concerned – the fact, that is, that he could not have left the line of cars if the other car had not backed up – it should be observed that Marino's statements on the point absolutely do not allow us to say that the Fiat 125 drove into the Simca, and therefore that the Simca had been in a transverse position, and in any case in a position such that it entirely blocked the Fiat 125, preventing it from leaving the parking place. Marino's statement that he could not leave the line of cars is not incompatible with the location of the dents, since it seems possible that, following the collision, the Fiat 125 came to be in a sort of bottleneck, since it had, on the one side, the front left section of the Simca 'pointing' at the front right wheel and, on the other, probably another parked car [the presence of which can be deduced from the fact that Marino states that he could not have left the line of cars if the Simca had not backed up, inasmuch as there was another car parked behind him, which leads us to suppose that there was another parked car on Marino's left, because otherwise it would have been sufficient for him to steer sharply to the left (that is, to back up slightly – and this would have been possible because, despite the fact that there was a car behind him, the Fiat 125 at the moment of the collision must have already advanced a few metres – and repeat the sharp left turn mentioned above) and drive away], so that it would not have been possible to leave the parking place without causing further damage, either to the Simca or to the other car, which could have been scraped by the left side of the Fiat 125, and in any

> case bringing about the exact effect that Marino wished to
> avoid – that of attracting attention to himself... (*Judge-*
> *ment*, pp. 279–80)

This laborious succession of subjunctives, conditionals, parentheses and brackets depicts an entirely fictitious landscape.
Parked cars, cars in motion, backing up and steering sharply
to the left – these are all hypothetical entities created by the
blind faith placed in Marino's reliability. This faith, apparently
proof against any risk of contradiction, induced the court (1)
to accept the conjecture proffered by Musicco on one important
point and, at the same time, to describe Musicco as 'unreliable
per se'; (2) to contradict at the same time, on a second point of
equal importance, both the drivers involved (at least according
to their accounts) in the accident; (3) to accept Marino's retrac-
tion on a third important point, while refusing to admit, in the
face of strong evidence to the contrary, that this was a retrac-
tion at all; (4) to set forth a welter of unfounded conjectures
concerning the movement of cars inside the parking lot near
the Via Cherubini on the morning of 17 May 1972. Couldn't
the court have avoided all this?

We have seen that the memoir drawn up by lawyer Pecorella (defence lawyer for Bompressi) offered an exceedingly
simple solution: Musicco's Simca never had a collision with the
Fiat 125 driven by the killers. The tests performed on the two
cars by the Police Forensic Division after the killing – according to the written judgement – would tend to exclude this
hypothesis. No one, as I shall shortly explain, is able to verify
this assertion fully at present. All the same, let us take it to be
so. There remains yet another possibility, which would immedi-

ately reconcile words and facts: the inconsistencies in Marino's account and the dents on the two cars. That morning, Musicco actually did have a collision with the Fiat 125 driven by the killers, but behind the wheel of that Fiat 125 was someone other than Marino.

(*f*) *Concerning the destruction of direct physical evidence.* The written judgement states that one of the items of proof of the collision between Musicco's Simca and the dark-blue Fiat 125 driven by the killers are the traces of dark-blue paint found by the Police Forensic Division on the bodywork of the Simca. In the memoir that has been mentioned repeatedly, lawyer Pecorella noted that this argument, in order to rise to the level of proof, would have required a comparative chemical and spectrographic analysis of the paint on the Fiat 125 and the traces of paint found on the Simca. This comparative analysis, however, according to the written judgement, 'is no longer possible' (*Judgement*, p. 262).

The reason is quite simple: the car driven by the killers had been destroyed in the meantime. Other equally important pieces of physical evidence – the clothing worn by Calabresi, one of the projectiles that struck him – have undergone the same fate (see above, Chapter XIV). The written judgement provides the bureacratic details of this incredible episode:

According to the inquiries ordered by the court, it appears that the vehicle was officially stricken from the PRA [*Public Registry of Automobiles – Translator's note*] because the car tax for the five-year period 1978–83 remained unpaid, and was demolished on 31 December 1988 [*The reader is urged to reread this phrase – Author's note*] . . .; the projectile was eliminated [*To be more exact, sold at auction due to lack of space – Author's note*] along with other evidence by Order of the Presiding Judge of the Court of Milan on 15 February 1987. . . .

As for Dottor Calabresi's clothing, it has been possible only to ascertain that the clothing was handed over to the chief police magistrate of Milan, along with his personal effects . . . (*Judgement*, p. 439)

In the written judgement, these actions are demurely referred to as 'administrative shortcomings'. An exceedingly mild statement, running a line and a half, deplores these 'shortcomings', and is followed by two-and-a-half typewritten pages arguing that the destruction of the evidence listed above was an act without substantial repercussions for the trial. The reasoning adduced in support of this position, unquestionably daring, should be read in its entirety:

Now, while we must agree with the criticism raised by the defence with respect to these administrative shortcomings, in terms of the trial it should be said that the failure to preserve the above-mentioned direct physical evidence, while deplorable, is not of such a nature as to undercut the body of evidentiary material acquired in the preliminary inquest and in court.

With respect to the Fiat 125, we have all the examinations and tests performed by the Police Forensic Division at the time, and not one but two expert examinations of the projectile were performed, establishing, as we have seen, the type of projectile, the type of cartridge upon which it was mounted and the origin of said cartridge, as well as the type of weapon from which it was fired; morphological and dimensional examinations were performed; the width and depth of the ridges cut into the projectile by the projections in the barrel of the weapon were measured, the type of antimony present was ascertained through neutron activation, for the purposes already stated.

Certainly, expert examinations can be repeated, records can be updated, as long as there is some useful purpose, some relevance to the trial.

With respect to the failure to assess physically the wind wing of the car, the subject of complaints by the defence, for example, Marino stated in court – before it had been determined that the Fiat 125 had been demolished – that he did not break the wind wing, but that he had 'popped' it out, and then replaced it, and that in this way the gasket, at the point where the screwdriver exerts pressure, sometimes breaks, and sometimes presents only a small mark, and in fact [*sic – Author's note*] the report drawn up by the Police Forensic Division makes no mention of the wind wing's having been forced.

Now, we cannot rule out that after eighteen years that small mark or that small fracture on the gasket might not still be detectable, even though it was not detected at the time; the spectrographic analysis of the paint might have supplied some useful element of information.

The truth is that proof (the result of proof), once it has been acquired and found suitable to demonstrate the existence of a fact or the guilt of a defendant, always has the same degree of efficacy, whether that proof is based on a single piece, or several pieces, of evidence, whether it is based on physical or documentary or critical or representative evidence.

If a fact is found to exist on the basis of a document or on the basis of testimony, the proof thus attained does not dwindle simply because it was not possible to examine another document or hear another witness.

One might respond that a certain document or a certain piece of testimony is insufficient to prove the existence of a fact, but if a document is found to be genuine, if a piece of testimony is considered to be reliable, if a proof is attained, then this piece of proof must have the same persuasive force as proof that is based upon numerous documents or numerous witnesses.

All that changes is the procedure to be followed in the evaluation of the proof: if it has only one source, the procedure must be more rigorous and every aspect must be evaluated; if there are numerous sources, the judge's task will be made easier.

Therefore, in the case under consideration, that Marino stole the car, that the car had a collision with Musicco's car, and that he [Marino] in the end took part in the murder are all certain, because his statements are borne out by numerous and reliable pieces of evidence, as we believe that we have shown in the preceding pages, to which we therefore refer the reader. (*Judgement*, pp. 440–42)

This argument can be broken down into three parts, which we shall discuss separately:

(*a*) The direct physical evidence could perfectly well be destroyed, because careful expert examinations had been conducted upon it.

(*b*) Other possible examinations might have led to some result.

(*c*) These results could not have contradicted the conclusions that had already been attained independently.

Point (*a*) seems implicitly to set forth a general principle. If we were to transfer it into the realm of historiography, this principle would authorize the destruction of all primary sources (chronicles, parliamentary records, medals, and so on and so forth) that had been the subject of a thorough historiographical treatment (the equivalent of an expert examination). One could use these absurd results to circumscribe still further the limits of the analogy between judge and historian. Every generation asks different questions of the past (and therefore, of the documents of the past), which cast new light on clearly established facts, as well (such as the storming of the Bastille, for instance), the existence of which no one would dream of disputing. Judges, on the other hand, deliver verdicts, valid here and now, on the basis of specific questions which may be modified over the course of a trial, but which in any case cannot be reformulated *ad infinitum*. All this is undoubtedly true, but is it appropriate to speak of a 'proof being attained', and therefore becoming (one presumes) definitive, when referring to a trial that has not yet been heard in an appeals court? 'Certainly, expert examinations can be repeated, records can be updated, as long as there is some useful purpose, some relevance to the trial,' the written judgement states: and the statement objectively sounds quite ironic, since in this trial certain expert examinations can no longer be repeated. It is clear that the possibility of asking new questions of the particular documentation constituted by the direct physical evidence has been lost once it has been destroyed.

Here we find point (*b*), which almost seems like a concession to the points made by the defence. The written judgement does not rule out the possibility that an examination of the gasket of the wind wing of the Fiat 125 might have led to the detection of a mark that had eluded the Police Forensic Division; it concedes that a spectrographic analysis of the paint of the Fiat 125 'might have supplied some useful element of information'. This means that the expert examinations of the past were not exhaustive: which is to say that they did not exhaust all the possible questions (and therefore, perhaps, all the possible answers).

And now we reach point (*c*), which immediately sets forth the limitations of these other expert examinations, which were never performed, and never can be. Whatever their findings, these examinations could never have undermined the 'proof attained'.

The foundation of this enormous confidence is not clear. Given the impossibility of performing a chemical and spectrographic analysis of the dark-blue paint of the Fiat 125 and the traces of dark-blue paint on Musicco's Simca, the written judgement asks us to settle for something less:

> . . . it is not clear why the presence of dark-blue paint on the Simca should be considered as being without probative value, as if at that time all cars were that colour.
>
> It may be something less than a conclusive element,

which has no decisive power because the car used in the assassination was not the only dark-blue car on the road in the Via Cherubini that morning, but it certainly cannot be considered *per se* an insignificant element. (*Judgement*, p. 264)

By relying upon analogous reasoning, as the reader will recall, every bank robber standing 1.8 metres tall involved in the robberies described by Marino was identified as Bompressi, and every bank robber with glasses was identified as Pedrazzini. 'If it has only one source', we read in the written judgement, 'the procedure [to be followed in evaluating evidence] must be more rigorous and every aspect must be evaluated.'

We have come back – as was inevitable – to the issue of the single source of proof, and therefore to Marino's reliability. In abstract terms it may be that, as we read in the written judgement, 'proof . . . always has the same degree of efficacy . . . whether it is based on physical or documentary or critical or representative evidence'. In concrete terms, however, different sources respond in different ways (and with varying degrees of thoroughness) to the same questions. This is certainly true for historians: the lives of the saints offer valuable information on the history of the countryside in the High Middle Ages, but they cannot take the place of the estate books that gave us, among other things, the name of Bodo (see above, Chapter XVIII). Judges, however, are also faced with similar difficulties, unless I am mistaken. In the trial we are discussing, the possibility of verifying Marino's statements on a number of decisive points – the weapon used in the murder, for example – was lost owing to the destruction of the direct physical evidence. The written judgement would have us believe that the Police Forensic Division performed all possible tests and analyses on the bullet, and reached unequivocal conclusions. In reality, the question is less straightforward. Marino stated that the pistol used was a Smith & Wesson long-barrel (which the written judgement states came from a stock of weapons stolen from the 'Marco Leone' gun shop in Turin). 'Two official expert examinations, conducted by experts of proven experience and reliability', concluded that the width of the imprints and the depth of the grooves on the bullet were compatible with only two types of pistol: Smith & Wesson .38 special and Hopkins & Allen (*Judgement*, p. 317). The two experts opted decisively for the Smith & Wesson. The defence, however, asked whether it were possible to infer the length of the pistol barrel (and therefore, the model of pistol) from the residue of unburnt powder on the bullet. One of the experts, Engineer Salza, did not rule that out, but he made it clear that the fact that he could never perform a new test on the bullet made it impossible to be certain:

> Well, I thought the problem over again. Perhaps, let us say, the presence of these residues depends on many factors, many variables, including also, I think, the length of the barrel. However, unfortunately, we no longer have access to the same cartridges, the same bullets. Frankly I have to say that, in short, the result would have insufficient value, let us say, to base a reliable judgement, a certain judgement, such as you naturally desire. More than anything else, it would have an indicative value. . . . (*Judgement*, p. 322)

The written judgement states that the pistol used to commit the murder was 'destined, of course, to be destroyed following the assassination (the very least sort of precaution that we can expect from anyone who sets out to murder a police superintendent' (*Judgement*, p. 317). A very reasonable statement. It is, however, truly deplorable that, in the meantime, the bullet fired from that pistol, the clothing that was pierced by that bullet, and the car in which the person who fired that pistol made his escape should all have been destroyed as well.

In the court's view all this, as we have seen, bears no relevance to the trial. That is a hyperbolic statement, comparable to an act of faith ('I believe you, Marino, so completely, that in exchange for your words I am willing to renounce all the direct physical evidence on earth'). One would expect a more sober attitude from a verdict in a murder trial.

(*g*) *Marino's reliability: the woman driving the car.* If Marino was the driver of the Fiat 125, then why is it that so many eyewitnesses saw a woman at the wheel? This inconsistency – not exactly marginal to the case – was discussed in dismissive terms in the written judgement, a written judgement that elsewhere is ineluctably prolix (*Judgement*, pp. 407–14; and see above, Chapter XV, *e*). Dal Piva and Pappini, for instance, who both claimed that the car was driven by a woman, are declared unreliable for the following reasons. Dal Piva, because she stated in court that she had seen two people get out of the Fiat 125 and *go towards* an Alfa Romeo Giulia: at that point (she said): 'I lowered my head, I raised it, and I no longer saw anyone.' Eighteen years before, immediately after the killing, she had stated instead that she saw the two people *get into* the Giulia:

'the inconsistency is so irremediable – according to the written judgement – that it reflects on all her testimony' (*Judgement*, p. 409) – which included, as the reader will recall, a minute description of the physique and clothing of the woman driving the Fiat 125. Pappini, on the other hand – convinced that the person driving the car was a woman, since that person had long hair – was considered unreliable because he was colour-blind: clearly, this invalidated his testimony concerning the colour of the hair (chestnut), but not its length.

The court, on the other hand, found Gnappi's testimony reliable; Gnappi had spoken of 'long and slightly wavy hair, like ... what can I say?, a lady's hair ... the hair was dark (very dark),' leading him to suppose that the killers' car was driven by a woman, or perhaps a hippie. The written judgement commented: 'Marino in court (pp. 127–8), before Gnappi's testimony, had stated that at the time he wore his hair "long ... very long, bushy, in other words", that his hair tended somewhat "to swell", and was somewhat "wavy" (see p. 2180)' (*Judgement*, p. 413).

I have previously referred briefly to the passage in which Marino in court described his own hair as 'bushy' (Chapter XV, *e*). Those words, however, were part of a complex inter-action comprising questions (from the presiding judge) and answers (from Marino) which is worth reproducing here:

Marino: 'My hair was long ... very long (bushy, in other words).'
Presiding judge: 'Bushy, or very long?'
Marino: 'Um ... very long. My hair, when it is long ...'
Presiding judge: 'Uh huh, you can see ...'

Marino: '. . . tends to . . .'

Presiding judge: '. . . to swell.'

Marino: '. . . to swell.'

Presiding judge: 'So you had a pile of hair?'

Marino: 'Yes.'

Presiding judge: 'A bit curly? Always like this, more or less?'

Marino: 'A bit wavy.'

Presiding judge: 'A bit wavy.' (*Trial*, pp. 127–8)

The written judgement speaks of 'a certain number of correspondences ("long" and "wavy" hair, colour of that hair) between the statements of Marino and the subsequent statements of Gnappi' (*Judgement*, pp. 412–13). In order to understand the reference to the 'subsequent statements', we should remember that Gnappi had *already* made a statement as one of the eyewitnesses immediately following the killing. The restrictive indication, 'a certain number of correspondences', however, is appropriate. The person at the wheel, Gnappi had said, 'was looking straight ahead and did not move, at least when I was looking at the car; I looked at that person for a moment, because I wanted to see them, but all I saw was a certain amount of hair.'

Another exchange between the presiding judge and Marino:

Presiding judge: 'I wanted to ask you: At that time, that is, 17 May – did you have a moustache?'

Marino: 'Yes, I had a moustache.'

Presiding judge: 'A visible moustache? A small one? Like . . .'

Marino: 'No, a very visible moustache.'

Presiding judge: 'A very visible moustache.'

One might well suppose that the person driving the Fiat 125 had no moustache, otherwise Gnappi would not have concluded that it was either a woman or a hippie.

(*b*) *Marino's reliability: the witnesses Pappini and Decio.* In the first section of this book, I quoted at length from the testimony of the witness Pietro Pappini, who – on the morning of the assassination – was driving along the Via Cherubini at the wheel of an Alfa Romeo 2000, just behind the Fiat 125 driven by the killers (see above, Chapter XV, subchapters *c*, *∂*). The written judgement quotes even longer passages from the same testimony (*Judgement*, pp. 381–90) to demonstrate Pappini's complete unreliability. Another witness, Margherita Decio, was reliable, on the other hand, in the court's opinion; at the wheel of a Bianchina, she was driving immediately behind Pappini's Alfa Romeo. Pappini's version and Decio's version were considered by the defence (and by this author: see above, Chapter XV, subchapter *c*) as substantially consistent, and inconsistent with the version given by Marino.

'This is not true,' the written judgement states, 'for the following reasons.' Let's hear those reasons:

Pappini speaks of a dark-blue Fiat 125 that 'was driving very slowly' (see *Police Report*, 17 May 1972); 'was moving pretty slowly' (*Police Report*, 25 May 1972); in court, after he stated that he had seen 'this car stopped there, and a man getting out, or getting in, now I can't remember,' he reiterates that the car was going 'slow', 'not fast' (pp. 905, 909, 913).

Decio, in court, speaks of a 'dark-blue Fiat 125 that was partly stopped, that is, that was going very slowly' (p. 1105), and says that 'between the first and the second shot, we were going very slowly, but we were going, and then we stopped' (p. 1106).

Now it hardly seems necessary to distinguish between 'slowly,' 'not fast', 'stopped', and 'partly stopped'; let us therefore admit, in accordance with the defence, that the two witnesses agree that the car was in motion.

What is important is to establish the moment from which the Fiat 125 was moving 'slowly', because it is one thing to say that the Fiat 125 was moving slowly (as Pappini says) before Calabresi crossed the street, before the Fiat 125 stopped to let the killer get out, etc., and it is quite another thing to say (as Decio says): ' . . . As soon as I turned into the Via Cherubini, I slowed down, because the car in front of me had slowed down, because in front of that car there was a dark-blue Fiat 125 that was partly stopped, that is, that was going very slowly. At that point, I heard a shot.'

In Decio's account, the succession of events is rapid: as soon as she turns into the Via Cherubini she slows down because the other car slows down; she seeks the cause of the slowdown (p. 1108) and sees the Fiat 125 partly stopped, or moving slowly; at this point, she hears a shot (p. 1105); she moves a few metres further and then hears another shot, and the cars stop.

There is no doubt that Pappini's 'moving slowly' (he

places it long before the shots – in fact Calabresi crosses the street, the car stops, the killer gets out and walks between the two cars, the Fiat 125 starts up again slowly, and only then does he hear the shots) and Decio's 'moving slowly' (just a few seconds before the second shot) have a completely different meaning.

Decio's version fits perfectly with Marino's account: 'At the very instant that Dottor Calabresi began to cross the street, I began to back the car up in order to be close, let us say, to the place where this was taking place, in order to make it possible for "Enrico" [= Bompressi] to get into the car without having to go very far, so I backed up and I must have gone . . . in reverse, I don't know, ten-fifteen metres . . . in short, far enough to reach, let us say more or less where this act was occurring, in other words' (*Transcript Courtroom Testimony*, p. 110). (*Judgement*, pp. 396–8)

By now the virtuoso interpretations of the author of the written judgement are well known to the reader. Concerning the accident in the parking lot, he considers Musicco to be unreliable and Marino reliable even where their versions (possibly both inaccurate on this point) coincide: 'In reality, the situations are entirely different.' Here Pappini is branded unreliable and Decio reliable, even though they are describing the same scene using the same words: 'There is no doubt that Pappini's "moving slowly" (he places it long before the shots – in fact Calabresi crosses the street, the car stops, the killer gets out and walks between the two cars, the Fiat 125 starts up again slowly, and only then does he hear the shots) and Decio's "moving slowly" (just a few seconds before the second shot) have a completely different meaning.'

And just what constitutes this enormous difference? In Decio's account, we are told, 'the succession of events is rapid', whereas the sequence is slowed in Pappini's account. This evaluation, however, fails to consider two elements – one general, the other specific: (1) to try to measure the respective duration of two series of events, lasting no more than a few seconds in any case, on the basis of two separate descriptions is evidently quite impossible; (2) Pappini, since he was closer to the car driven by the killers, noted and described a greater number of events, giving the impression of a slower sequence; Decio described a smaller number of events because her view was partially blocked by Pappini's Alfa Romeo 2000 (see above, Chapter XV, subchapter *c*).

Where the explicator outdoes himself, however, is in his statement that 'Decio's version fits perfectly with Marino's account'. It fits so imperfectly that it leaves a gaping and spectacular hole: Marino's claim that he drove the Fiat 125 backwards for ten or fifteen metres. As I have already noted (Chapter XV, subchapter *c*), the fact that he backed up the car escaped the notice not only of Decio, but also of all those present. The written judgement observes that their versions (with the exception of Pappini's version) do not point 'in the opposite direction from the backing up described by Marino' (*Judgement*, p. 381). The reader will agree that there is a considerable difference between 'not pointing in the opposite direction' and the 'fitting perfectly' attributed to Decio's account. If we really need to talk about anything fitting perfectly, then we should apply that term to the unanimous chorus of silence that the witnesses (including Decio) offer concerning Marino's driving in reverse a few seconds before the killing.

In court, faced with the defence's objections concerning this point, Marino replied clumsily, saying, among other things: 'At the time when I was backing up, no shots had yet been fired, and so nobody noticed ... the fact that I was backing up.'

In the written judgement, these words are commented on as follows:

> How should Marino have behaved in the face of these objections?
>
> He was asked a question, and he replied, attempting to offer an explanation of that contrast, and to tell the truth, he supplied a plausible explanation.
>
> Should he simply have not answered? (*Judgement*, pp. 401–2)

We should ask another question, actually. For the umpteenth time in the course of this trial, the only corroboration of Marino's words is offered by Marino himself.

(*i*) *Reliable and unreliable witnesses: the thunderstorm and the procession.* As we have seen, the certificates of reliability awarded to Marino in the written judgement are numerous. The other defendants, and the witnesses called by the defence, are repeatedly dismissed as 'unreliable', 'not credible', and so on. I would like to show the basis for those judgements, and the consequences that ensued. I shall limit my analysis to two points in the trial: (*a*) the conversation in front of a café in Pisa, on 13 May 1972, in which Sofri, at the end of a rally which he addressed, supposedly urged Marino to kill Calabresi; (*b*) the congratulations for good work that Sofri supposedly gave Marino, immediately prior to addressing another rally in the Piazza degli Aranci at Massa on 20 May 1972. Both circumstances, which would prove that Sofri ordered the killing, are of course known to us from a single source: Marino.

I will begin with the first circumstance, which is also the most important. During the confrontation, at the time of the preliminary inquest (16 September 1988), Sofri said that on the evening of 13 May 1972, while he was in the company of other people in the home of his ex-wife, Marino came to call on him; he added that he had remembered this evening meeting right from his first interrogation (which took place on 3 August 1988), during which he had foretold important revelations. He had, however, failed to mention the circumstance because, he said, 'during that first interrogation I still believed that in the confrontation Marino would tell the truth' (*Judgement*, p. 512).

'Improbable statements,' comments the written judgement, 'and rightly the plaintiffs observe that there might well have been no confrontation. . . . One might say – but it was not said – that Sofri might well have thought that mentioning that circumstance could in some way hurt him, and the defendant has no obligation to provide evidence to the prosecution, and so he reasonably enough failed to mention it' (*Judgement*, p. 513).

This is a wholly gratuitous insinuation. An evening meeting at a home makes the meeting described by Marino improbable, meaning that he preferred to speak about a planned murder not only in public, but in a place crowded with policemen. It is not clear why the court should have considered with suspicion – as if it were evidence of guilt – the fact that Sofri should at first have said nothing about seeing Marino on the evening of 13 May 1972 at his ex-wife's home. Marino had completely forgotten this circumstance – he admitted it only once it had been mentioned by Sofri. But Marino's forgetfulness (much like his sloppiness) was taken by the court as a confirmation of his reliability (note the written judgement, p. 157, concerning Marino's mistaken orientation on the street map: above, Chapter III).

In the face of Marino's accusations concerning a supposed conversation that took place sixteen years earlier, Sofri immediately proclaimed his innocence, excluding in the most absolute terms the fact that the conversation in question had ever occurred. (That Sofri, once the preliminary inquest had begun, should have expected a rapid confrontation with his accuser should come as a surprise to no one.) That was not all, however; Sofri went further, producing a series of arguments that rendered that conversation following the rally not impossible, certainly, but unlikely: the thunderstorm, which had coincided with the end of the rally, and the meeting with Marino on the evening of 13 May (as mentioned above). Sofri remembered that he had talked with various comrades from Tuscany, immediately after the end of the rally, concerning the possibility of erecting a plaque in honour of Franco Serantini; he then drove off with Guelfi, a Lotta Continua militant, to see a mutual friend, Soriano Ceccanti, whom he had met briefly during the procession that had preceded the demonstration (see above,

Chapter XVII). There was no room for the supposed dialogue with Marino in this series of events.

Many former Lotta Continua militants who had taken part in the demonstration on 13 May 1972 confirmed in court, eighteen years later, the circumstances described by Sofri. In court, testimony was heard concerning a 'thunderstorm', a 'heavy shower', and 'heavy rain'; photographs were shown from that day (ignored in the written judgement), documenting extensive use of umbrellas by the demonstrators. Luciano Della Mea, who was with Mughini in another piazza in Pisa where Giancarlo Pajetta was delivering a speech, said that he remembered that day 'quite vividly, because Mughini was wearing leather, and the water was streaming down that shiny leather, and so it was a really heavy and lengthy storm'.

'Now,' we read in the written judgement, 'that it started raining during the rally is true. It is equally true, however, that it did not rain with the intensity that the defendant and the above witnesses would like us to believe.'

The Special Office of the Civil Engineering Corps for the Hydrographic Service of Pisa stated that on that day there was 1.2 millimetres of precipitation; the Office for Aviation Telecommunications, the meteorological service for Rome, says that in the late afternoon there was a 'light continuous rain' in Pisa, followed in the evening by a 'light intermittent rain'. In short, it was raining, but not heavily (even though the newspapers that published articles about the rally mentioned, 'driving rain' and 'heavy rain'). And so, according to the court, Guelfi, Ceccanti, and all the witnesses who speak of thunderstorms, and so on, are unreliable. Exceedingly reliable, on the other hand, was Dottor Ignazio Tronca, formerly chief of political police in

Pisa, who – after errors and forgetfulness concerning the date of the rally, where it occurred, and so on – stated in court that the demonstrators first 'gathered in dribs and drabs' in front of the institute where Serantini had lived, then 'went to the piazza in small bunches, and maybe even in crowded groups, but in short, not in a procession' (*Judgement*, pp. 551–2). Thus, the written judgement concluded, 'with reference to the conversation in Pisa with Sofri', Marino's statements 'remain intact, since the entire version offered by the defence – with a view to depicting the course of that demonstration in a certain manner, a manner whereby there was no space whatever for a conversation between Sofri and Marino following the rally – has been refuted' (*Judgement*, pp. 612–13).

It was raining, but not hard; therefore Marino told the truth about his conversation with Sofri; the demonstrators went to the rally 'maybe even in crowded groups,' but not in a 'procession "proper"' (Tronca: *Judgement*, p. 552); therefore Sofri ordered the murder of Calabresi. How was it possible to create this logical monstrosity? A memorable page of the written judgement explains:

Without the procession and the thunderstorm, another demonstration emerges: the piazza and the stage are fully prepared, the first militants arrive and begin to hang around, others arriving in smaller or larger groups, all waiting for the scheduled hour to arrive; the piazza is filling up, the leaders and the speakers are arriving or are already there; it is possible for one and all to say hello to them or chat with them, and then the rally begins, the first speakers open the demonstration, Sofri concludes it, the crowd begins to leave the piazza; once again it is possible for one and all, militants, sympathizers, national and local leaders, those from other cities, to approach the stage and the speakers.

Without that thunderstorm, the picture of Sofri and Guelfi leaving the piazza alone after a demonstration of that type is unreal.

... There is evidence that this demonstration did not occur as it has been depicted by the defendant and the witnesses called by the defence.

Now, if one person and another supply a version designed to offer a reconstruction of an event in such a way that there is no room for the meeting described by Marino, and we then find that this reconstruction is a false depiction of reality, with a view specifically to eliminating the possibility of such a meeting, all this, in the court's view, constitutes evidence, another element of proof, which confirms that the meeting did occur after the rally. . . . (*Judgement*, pp. 614–15)

Now, just why the scene of Sofri and Guelfi leaving the site of the rally should be 'unreal' is not clear: after all, we know that most of Lotta Continua's national leadership was not in Pisa that day. The written judgement observes that Sofri and the others 'all account for each other's presence in turn' (to be exact, nine witnesses mention a total of fifteen names) – a mean-spirited observation that seems to hint at some prearranged agreement (*Judgement*, p. 540). If they were all there, however, it seems inevitable that they would mention each other. What is important to note, however, is the conclusion of the passage quoted immediately above: 'Another element of proof'. The first element, I suppose, would be Marino's statement. Therefore, the *possibility* that Marino and Sofri spoke to each other proves that they actually did speak. This new logical pratfall is based on the premiss that the reconstruction provided by the witnesses called by the defence was not, let us say, inaccurate, but false ('false depiction of reality'). This is a premiss that remains groundless or, if demonstrated, demonstrated fallaciously. Let one example suffice.

The witness Lazzerini, after describing the demonstration at Pisa ('There was an assembly point near the station; from the station we moved along the Corso Italia and we arrived, after crossing the river Arno, near the Piazza San Silvestro . . .') pronounced the forbidden word 'procession' ('It was drizzling during the procession'); shortly thereafter he went so far as to speak of 'a real . . . downpour' falling towards the end of the rally. For these faults, the written judgement immediately identifies him as an unreliable witness (*Judgement*, pp. 618–19). Lazzerini, however, also testified that he had met Ovidio Bompressi in Massa, where he lived and still lives, on 17 May 1972, at around 12.25 p.m. – this testimony, while not constituting an alibi in the truest sense of the word, still makes it unlikely that at 9.15 a.m. on the same day Bompressi was in the Via Cherubini in Milan, murdering Luigi Calabresi (*Judgement*, p. 617). Now, the fact that Lazzerini testified (see the written judgement, pp. 619–20) 'to a circumstance, the procession in Pisa, which never took place' simply constitutes 'a further element of proof against Bompressi'. And even though the procession in Pisa is not

> essential to the defendant Bompressi, it should be observed that this circumstance shows that there is a link between the witnesses called by Bompressi and the (numerous) witnesses summoned by the defendant Sofri who also testify to the same event, which never took place. And if there is a connection between the witnesses summoned by one and the other defendant ... it is evident that we have gone beyond the simple failure to demonstrate innocence through proper exercise of the right to self-defence, and we have entered the field of activity directed towards the evasion of penal justice.

Once again, it is difficult, as one reads these words, not to think of the attitude of judges in witch trials: one of those trials which, on the strength of a single confession, wound up drawing into its coils all the inhabitants of an entire village. One wonders how close we came to seeing not merely all the defence witnesses but all the former Lotta Continua militants in Pisa and Massa indicted for perjury, or even worse. Now I am not questioning the good faith of the judges of the court – but it seems clear to me that in this case the bounds of reasonable procedure have been amply violated. To draw iron-bound deductions from a wavering premiss is always a dangerous thing. The abrupt statement that the procession in Pisa is something 'which never took place' clashes even with the cautious courtroom statements of Dottor Tronca – a witness who is highly praised in the written judgement.

Presiding judge: 'Now as to the stream of people arriving in the piazza where the procession took place, do you remember, as chief of the Political Office, whether they arrived in any particular fashion, in a group, in an organized procession, or do you not remember, or do you exclude that?'

Tronca: 'Well . . . an organized procession . . . I *would rule that out*; I *don't remember any such thing*; in any case, I *would rule that out*. In that context, *it does not seem to me* that there was a preceding procession that streamed . . . that had streamed into the piazza. *I don't believe so*. I think that . . . yes, I remember that the demonstrators went to the piazza in small bunches, and maybe even in crowded groups, but in short, not in a procession.'

'Statements that leave no doubt concerning the fact that there was no procession,' comments the written judgement (p. 553). The conditionals and the 'I-don't-think-so's' that I have put in italics seem to indicate an initial uncertainty, which was then resolved in the distinction between 'crowded groups' and 'procession'. In any case, a distinction of this sort implies a continuum, not a stark distinction, like that between a man or a woman at the wheel (just to stay within the context of the trial; I am excluding, for ease of discussion, the issue of hermaphrodites). To associate criminal intent with any and all mention of a procession by a witness truly seems beyond the pale. Actually, the testimony of those who took part in the demonstration (including Marino, who spoke during the preliminary inquest of an 'enormous demonstration') clearly indicates that there was a procession that day in Pisa. Even the possible absence of a 'full-fledged' procession (to use the words of Dottor

Tronca) would not prove that Sofri met Marino after the rally, outside a café, in order to persuade him, in a conversation that lasted just a few minutes, to go to Milan and kill Calabresi.

In connection with the congratulations that Sofri is alleged to have extended to Marino in the Piazza degli Aranci in Massa on 20 May 1972, there is even less to be said. Sofri mentioned an episode, also confirmed by two witnesses (Pegollo and Tognini), which occurred immediately before the rally – Dottor Costantino, then chief of the Political Office in Massa, had given him official warning not to speak of Calabresi. In court, Costantino confirmed that he had met Sofri at the end of the rally. About the official warning given to Sofri prior to the rally, on the other hand, he said that he was quite uncertain:

> Judge, it may be . . . however, I honestly could not say for sure. It may be that before the rally we exchanged a few words, but. . . . Afterwards, I can remember quite clearly, but beforehand, to be honest, I cannot. That is, I cannot rule that out. I don't remember . . . I don't think so. I don't think so. But I cannot rule it out to a certainty. . . . I think that I can rule it out, because we had already warned him in police headquarters. And he had given us the greatest assurances. . . . That is, I do not remember, Judge. It may be, but I really don't think so.

The uncertainty of this witness is perfectly comprehensible – after all, eighteen years have gone by. But for the court, he 'contradicted the version of the defendant and that of the witnesses Pegollo and Tognini'. Of course, these latter witnesses were then declared unreliable. The testimony of Costantino 'has become an element supporting the case of the prosecution' (*Judgement*, p. 563). Costantino cannot remember, or, better still, 'feels that he can rule it out' – therefore Marino is telling the truth.

On this sort of foundation, 'in the name of the Italian people' (and therefore in my name, and in the name of the readers of the original edition of this book), the Milan Court of Assizes sentenced Adriano Sofri to twenty-two years in prison.

AFTERWORD:
TWO VERDICTS COMPARED

1. On 22 January 1997, the Supreme Court of Italy took under examination the petition against the verdict of the Milan Court of Appeal which had convicted and sentenced – on 11 November 1995 – Adriano Sofri, Giorgio Pietrostefani and Ovidio Bompressi to twenty-two years in prison, for the crimes of ordering (the first two) and physically committing (the third) the murder of Police Superintendent Luigi Calabresi, killed in Milan on 17 May 1972. The same verdict acquitted – for expiration of the statute of limitations – their accuser, Leonardo Marino, who claimed that he had driven the getaway car used in the killing. The petition presented by Bompressi, Pietrostefani and Sofri was rejected; the convictions and sentences handed down by the Milan Court of Appeal became operative. Taking into account the ages of Bompressi, Pietrostefani, and Sofri – between fifty and fifty-five – these are life sentences.

This, then, was the conclusion – after nine years and seven verdicts – of a legal case without precedent in Italy – and, perhaps, outside Italy too.

2. Seven verdicts in nine years. Here is a list, specifying in each case the outcome for the chief defendants:

(i) Court of Assizes of Milan (2 May 1990): Sofri, Pietrostefani and Bompressi sentenced to 22 years; Marino to 11 years;

(ii) Court of Appeal of Milan (2 July 1991): Sofri, Pietrostefani and Bompressi sentenced to 22 years; Marino to 11 years;

(iii) Supreme Court of Italy, United Penal Sections (23 October 1992): previous verdict struck down for grave faults of method and logic;

(iv) first petition to the Court of Appeal of Milan (21 December 1993): acquittal of all the leading defendants;

(v) Supreme Court of Italy, First Penal Section (27 October 1994): previous verdict struck down for formal faults;

(vi) second petition to the Court of Appeal of Milan (11 November 1995): Sofri, Pietrostefani and Bompressi sentenced to 22 years; Marino acquitted for expiration of the statute of limitations;

(vii) Supreme Court of Italy, Fifth Penal Section (22 January 1997): previous verdict upheld.

What explanation can be offered for the fact that the Milan Court of Appeal should, over the course of four years, have successively convicted, acquitted, and reconvicted the same defendants? What explanation can there be for three radically different verdicts handed down by the Supreme Court of Italy?

3. To answer these questions, we must revisit the various phases of this exceedingly intricate affair, beginning with the

trial that ended with verdict (i). In my original book, *Il giudice e lo storico*, I analysed the records of the trial, and concluded that (a) Marino is not credible; and (b) that the only evidence against the other three defendants were Marino's accusations.

I shall come back to point (b) in the pages that follow. As far as point (a) is concerned, I observed that Marino is not credible primarily because the circumstances of his repentance and confession, which occurred sixteen years after the murder, are shrouded in mystery. His collaboration with the law supposedly began (according to the first official version) on 20 July 1988. During the course of the first trial, it emerged instead that Marino's night-time meetings with the *carabinieri* in the Sarzana barracks had begun at least as early as 2 July. Investigating Magistrate Pomarici was forced to admit that he had at first given an inaccurate date. Why had he done so? What did Marino and the *carabinieri* say to each other during those night-time meetings, of which there are naturally no records? And why did *carabinieri* colonel Nobili – during a press conference held on 28 July 1988, immediately following the arrest of Sofri, Pietrostefani and Bompressi – state repeatedly that contact with Marino had begun 'several months ago'? And how can we believe the official version, repeated (with numerous unpersuasive details) in court, according to which a high-ranking officer of the *carabinieri*, Colonel Bonaventura, who had long been working on the Calabresi case, hurried in the middle of the night from Milan to Sarzana to hear the confessions of a humble crêpe vendor (Marino) who continued to speak in vague terms of a 'grave occurrence' – an occurrence that was only later identified as the murder of Calabresi?

Marino is not credible because his testimony is full of

mistakes. He was wrong about the colour of the car he drove to the scene of the crime (dark blue, not beige); he was wrong about the route used in the getaway; he was wrong about a meeting with one of the supposed instigators of the crime (Pietrostefani), with whom he said he spoke in Pisa following a political rally – only to change his mind, eliminating him from the scene when it was pointed out to him that during the period in question, Pietrostefani would hardly have appeared in public because he was wanted by the police. And that is not all: Marino's version differs in many points from the testimony of eyewitnesses who were at the scene of the crime. None of them remembers a car backing up, as Marino claims to have done immediately after the shooting; many of the witnesses saw a woman driving the killers' car – some described her in detail – and not a man (i.e. Marino); the witness Musicco described a minor collision with a car (perhaps the killers' car) in terms quite different from those used by Marino – who then changed his version during the course of the trial.

In the light of all these facts, it is difficult to consider that Marino's self-accusations are proven. The accusations he levels against Sofri, Bompressi and Pietrostefani – as I have shown at length – are certainly not proven. None the less, the judges of the Milan Court of Assizes believed Marino in the face of everyone and everything: inconsistencies, corrections, refutations. In cases of inconsistency between eyewitnesses to the murder and Marino, Marino's version was held to be closer to the truth.

4. The appeals trial, which ended with verdict (ii), followed the logic of the first trial, but inserting a new point into the

written judgement: even independently of Marino's testimony, the existence had been proved – within the group Lotta Continua – of a clandestine terrorist structure, which ordered and carried out the assassination of Police Superintendent Calabresi.

These and other conclusions were harshly criticized in verdict (iii), handed down by the United Penal Sections of the Supreme Court of Italy. The petition against the verdict of the Milan Court of Appeal was at first assigned to the First Section of the Supreme Court; later, to the Sixth Section. The wholly exceptional decision to submit the petition to the United Penal Sections of the Supreme Court – a decision that involved the whole of the highest court of law in the Italian system of justice – was made in order to find some way of resolving a jurisprudential disagreement among the various sections. This disagreement concerned a crucial point: the exact meaning of the 'other elements of proof', or corroboration, without which, according to the Italian penal code, an accusation of complicity has no value. According to one persuasion, these elements of corroborative evidence must 'refer to facts that directly attach to the person of the defendant in connection with the specific crime of which he is accused', they must 'be open to interpretation solely as confirmation of the charges', and they must concern 'all of the crimes with which the defendant is charged, not only some of them'. According to another orientation, these elements of proof 'need not directly concern the actual crime with which the defendant is charged, inasmuch as they serve only to confirm *ab extrinseco* the reliability of the person accusing them of complicity'; therefore, 'these elements of proof may be only logical in nature, or they may concern only some of the defendants or some of the crimes described by the accuser [of complicity]' (written judgement of the United Penal Sections of the Supreme Court, 23 October 1992, hereafter referred to as SU, p. 43). The United Sections clearly chose the first and more rigorous orientation – even though, as we shall see, many of the 'errors of a methological nature, shortcomings, and faults' found in 'many and decisive points' in the verdict of the Court of Appeal (SU, p. 45) would have been equally open to censure in the light of the second orientation, far less demanding in terms of evidence and proof.

The verdict of the United Sections concluded:

Obviously, the judge who will retry this case – in the fullness of his discretionary powers – must completely re-evaluate the complex whole of the trial's findings, in accordance with proper judicial and methodological principles, and with a logical and consistent approach, free to reach the same conclusions as were produced by the verdict we have struck down, but through an appropriate logical and judicial process. (SU, p. 131)

We can read, between the lines of this verdict, the faults attributed to the previous verdict, which the Supreme Court was annulling: that verdict employed improper judicial and methodological principles, and followed an illogical and inconsistent approach. The Milan Court of Appeal re-examined the case, with these instructions in mind. Verdict (iv) concluded with the acquittal of the defendants, with a majority vote (according to a rumour that has never been denied) by the jury of the people, against the advice of the magistrate/jurors.

That could not stand. The assistant judge who drew up the written judgement of the verdict put together what is known in the parlance of the Italian legal profession as a 'suicide judgement', written in such a patently illogical manner that it automatically left itself open to annulment on the grounds of formal faults. (This sort of procedure may be technically impeccable – but what should we think of a legal system that endorses it?) A long disquisition on the reliability of Marino's confessions – followed by four short pages listing the dubious points of those confessions – could hardly help but be struck down by the Supreme Court. And that is precisely what happened, following a routine petition (verdict [v]). This brings us to a new verdict, the sixth, which overturned the findings of the fourth verdict, confirming the convictions of the first trial.

The verdict that closed the case (vii) rejected the petition against verdict (vi), declaring repeatedly, as was obligatory, that it was based upon the methodological principles set forth by the United Sections (iii) in overturning verdict (ii). In order to see whether this was the case – and, if so, in what terms – allow me to inspect carefully a number of essential points (a complete examination would require far too much room). In order to facilitate the comparison between the two verdicts of the Supreme Court, I have italicized the excerpts from the verdict of the United Sections (indicated with the abbreviation SU), and left in normal type the excerpts from the verdict of the Fifth Penal Section (indicated simply as Fifth Section).

5. In a case of this sort, based upon an accusation of complicity, it is necessary to establish the (a) overall and (b) intrinsic

credibility of the person accusing others of being his partners in crime. Is Marino credible in general terms? The verdict of the United Sections cast doubt on that question:

> *The very decision to confess after sixteen years to a grave episode of terrorism, levelling accusations against one's accomplices – considered in and of itself – has a number of ambiguous and disquieting potential aspects, which certainly deserved* [from the judges of the Milan Court of Appeal – Author's note] *a more thorough and complete consideration.* (SU, p. 54)

Marino could have been prompted, the verdict of the United Sections went on, by 'a dangerous desire for vengeance' against such former leaders of Lotta Continua as Sofri and Pietrostefani who, after the end of their shared political activity, had enjoyed much easier lives than Marino. And then there was the question of the robberies, committed by Marino almost right up to the eve of his 'repentance':

> *the voided verdict has also failed to respond thoroughly to the question of how to reconcile the image of a good and resigned man with this same man's willingness to engage in armed robberies until just a short while before confiding in the parish priest, armed robberies that were certainly no longer prompted by political ideals, but merely by a thirst for money, pursued in an aggressive and dangerous manner.* (SU, p. 55)

Now let us hear the Fifth Section of the Supreme Court. The 'image of a good man in the throes of remorse and that of a man who, long after his involvement in political activities, and until just a short time prior to his confession to the parish priest, commits robberies for personal gain' are entirely compatible: Marino's remorse was circumscribed, and concerned only that 'particularly grave occurrence', that is, the killing of Calabresi. He had previously considered the robberies as 'nothing more than legitimate proletarian expropriations and therefore nothing that could prompt particular problems with his conscience'. Verdict (vi) (the Fifth Section went on) then specified 'logically . . . as a demonstration that the robberies were not part of Marino's personality, that he – ever since his father's death, when he was still a youth – "never failed for even a day" to work honestly, for himself and for his family' (Fifth Section, pp. 49–50).

Thus, the fact that the robber Marino was an honest worker demonstrates 'logically' that the robberies were not part of his personality. A strange – let us even say dangerous – logic proffered by the Fifth Section. But there is more to come.

6. Let us move on to Marino's intrinsic credibility, beginning with the accusation levelled against Sofri.

Marino said that he had been urged to kill Calabresi during a short conversation that took place in a café, or – in a later version – in the street, following a rally led by Sofri himself in Pisa on 13 May 1972. Sofri rejected out of hand the existence of such a conversation, adding that in any case the circumstances described by Marino made that conversation highly unlikely. In fact, (a) on that 13 May 1972 in Pisa there was a 'downpour'; (b) the cafés in the area, given the rally and the tension in the city, were all closed; (c)

Marino would have been able to speak safely with Sofri in the home of Sofri's ex-wife, where he actually came to visit, in the company of others, that same evening. It later emerged from a series of inquiries that it had indeed rained in Pisa on that 13 May 1972 (there are photographs that show the audience listening to Sofri's speech under a forest of open umbrellas), but that there had not been a 'downpour'; and some cafés had stayed open. Verdict (ii) (adhering to the previous verdict in this detail) interpreted these divergences in accordance with a form of logic that earned it a stern reprimand from the United Sections:

The voided verdict observes on page 240 that Marino's account is detailed and consistent, and not adequately undermined by the factual elements adduced by the defence to discredit that account, elements that in the final analysis were shown to be false.

At this point – the verdict observes verbatim, on page 241 – 'there can be only one consequence: if one denies a fact, supporting the denial with statements which then prove to be false, then the denial is also false and the fact that was denied is true'.

Such a principle must be rejected out of hand as it is clearly in conflict with the rule that the burden of proof is on the prosecution (which derives from the constitutional principle of the presumption of innocence, article 27, clause 2 of the Italian Constitution).

The mendacious statement of the defendant, set forth to dispute a statement proffered by the prosecution, is used to establish decisive proof of that statement, with an aphorism reading roughly, you lie and therefore you are guilty. (SU, pp. 77–8)

An observation. To speak of a 'mendacious statement' on the part of the defendant, as does the verdict of the United Sections, is entirely inappropriate: Sofri's statements concerning the rain and the cafés are minor inaccuracies, easily understandable sixteen years after the fact; the statement concerning Marino's visit to the home of Sofri's ex-wife is a fact that even Marino (who entirely failed to mention it in his first testimony) never dreamed of contradicting. Still, the methodological indications offered by the United Sections are sound. In the same spirit, I had written, ironically mimicking the aberrant logic of the Milanese judges: 'It was raining, but not hard; therefore Marino told the truth about his conversation with Sofri ...' (see above, p. 178).

Let us now see how the Fifth Section evaluated these methodological indications. After emphasizing that the meeting between Marino and Sofri 'could not be ruled out by the testimony of the witnesses concerning Sofri's movements', the Fifth Section observed that this served 'evidently, only to exclude that there is any proof of a "non-meeting", and therefore a corresponding unreliability of Marino' (Fifth Section, pp. 93–4).

This might seem to be an obvious statement: it is clear that the demonstration of the nonexistence of the meeting would also demonstrate the unreliability of Marino. As the United Sections emphasized, however, the burden of proof is on the prosecution. It is the meeting that must be proved, not the non-meeting. The Fifth Section placed the burden of proof upon Sofri, paying absolutely no attention to the unequivocal instructions of the United Sections.

The nonexistence of the proof of the non-meeting, however, does not yet demonstrate that Marino is specifically reliable. This was stated, with observations demonstrating elementary good sense, by the United Sections: *'The question of whether the meeting recalled by Marino actually took place or not does not complete the investigation bent on ascertaining the guilt or innocence of the defendant accused of complicity, because it is also necessary to determine whether the subject of the conversation that took place during that meeting was that of ordering a murder'* (SU, p. 84). Some corroboration, some evidence, is required. And here it is. It takes the form, no more and no less, of Marino's presence at the rally where Sofri spoke, in Pisa, on 13 May 1972. In the view of the Fifth Section, this constitutes objective corroboration of Sofri's guilt (Fifth Section, pp. 94–5), and the observations made in the verdict of the Milan Court of Appeal were 'certainly logical':

It was surely neither 'normal nor routine' for Marino to be present in Pisa, requiring a 400-kilometre journey, for a demonstration that was predominantly local and Tuscan in nature (a commemoration of the death of the student Serantini), where it would appear that no other Piedmontese or Lombard militants took part, considering moreover that Marino had had no interactions with Sofri for more than a year, and that the meeting took place just a few days prior to the killing of Calabresi.

'Certainly logical!' This is a logic that we have seen before: Marino went from Turin to Pisa to hear a speech by Sofri, therefore Sofri ordered the murder of Calabresi; Marino had not seen Sofri for over a year, therefore Sofri ordered the murder of Calabresi; Marino heard a speech by Sofri just a few days after the murder of Calabresi, therefore Sofri ordered the murder of Calabresi. 'And equally logically,' the verdict of the Fifth Section continues, unperturbed, 'Marino's presence in Massa for Sofri's speech at the rally of 20 May 1972 was recognized as a corroborative element; that indeed, these two "anomalous" presences "bracketing" the killing of Calabresi logically underscore the already considerable corroborative value that either presence possesses on its own' (Fifth Section, pp. 122–3). As the reader can see, since it was impossible to prove that Sofri gave Marino (a) an order to kill Calabresi, following the rally in Pisa; or (b) congratulations for the successful killing, prior to the rally in Massa, the judges of the Fifth Section of the Supreme Court were satisfied with something less: Marino's presence (along with about a thousand others) in Pisa and in Massa.

We have already seen this probatory approach in the verdict of the Court of Appeal (ii), which therefore incurred a stern reprimand from the United Sections:

> *In the corroboration of the order to commit murder – denounced by Marino – reliance was placed upon two clearly illegitimate principles, stating 'in primis' that the difficulty of proving moral complicity legitimizes, by that difficulty alone, the acceptance of a sort of 'probatio semiplena'.*
>
> *As a result, reliance was placed upon generic elements of evidence, such as the visits between Pietrostefani and Marino in Turin and elsewhere, or the meeting between Sofri and Marino after the rally in Pisa on 13 May 1972 and the later meeting prior to the rally in Massa on the 20th of the same month.* (SU, pp. 49–50)

As we have seen, the Fifth Section blithely overlooked this stern criticism of illegitimate reasoning.

7. Let us move on to the accusations against Pietrostefani. The United Sections had found that in Marino's testimony:

> *there is no shortage of errors, inconsistencies, corrections, and progressive adjustments, often correlated with objections from the co-defendants that Marino was accusing of complicity; the problem posed by all this, however, was solved simply and substantially by referring to the length of time that has gone by since the events occurred (this circumstance, however, was not taken into consideration in evaluating the reliability of the witnesses called by the defence, nor for the witnesses summoned by the prosecution, when their testimony failed, in whole or in part, to correspond with Marino's version).* (SU, p. 47)

The Milan Court of Appeal (verdict [vi]) replied by observing that the 'errors, inconsistencies, etc.' were 'inaccuracies of only marginal importance, absolutely insufficient to undermine the credibility of Marino's account, considering its complexity, the length of time that had passed, and the fact that Marino is not an intellectual' (Fifth Section, pp. 46–7). In truth, the inaccuracies in Marino's account have to do with points that are anything but marginal; and it is not clear why his memory on these points should have anything to do with what diplomas and degrees he holds. Even the judges of the Milan Court of Appeal, however, in all their paternalistic demagoguery, were forced to recognize that 'the correction concerning Pietrostefani's presence in Pisa on 13 May 1972' constituted a separate case. They justified it by 'noting that the gradual corrections had not been the consequence of specific objections by the co-defendants, who in that period had not only not been heard from but had not yet even been arrested, nor of new findings of the court, but were merely the result of efforts to remember by the witness/defendant [i.e. Marino] in the context of what may be considered a single act split up into several interrogations' (Fifth Section, p. 47).

These statements, recklessly accepted and incorporated by the Fifth Section (Fifth Section, p. 90), are barefaced falsehoods. Anyone who bothers to read the appropriate passages in the preliminary inquest and the courtroom testimony can see this (see above, pp. 25–32). Marino changed his version following the objections of Pietrostefani in the preliminary inquest, he changed it again following the confrontation with Sofri during the preliminary inquest, and he changed it once again during the courtroom testimony in the Court of Assizes. There, Marino finally ejected Pietrostefani from the scene once and for all. 'Pietrostefani was not there at that moment, I did not see him, and I do not remember him being there' (see above, p. 31).

Still, the verdict of the Court of Appeal (verdict [vi]) emphasized 'for the sake of completeness' – it is the Fifth Section which notes this – that if there was no proof of the presence of Pietrostefani in Pisa on 13 May 1972, there was also no certainty of his absence from the said city on that day' (Fifth Section, p. 90). It is the usual logic (if we can call it that): the burden of proof rests – in this case, 'for the sake of completeness' – upon the accused, rather than upon the prosecution, as the law requires. This procedure, which is objectionable *per se*, is absolutely senseless here. Why should Pietrostefani be required to prove that he was not in Pisa on 13 May 1972, when it is none other than his accuser, Marino, who denies his presence, with an about-face that, taken alone, should have been enough to demolish his credibility? And above all, what does any of this have to do with the accusation – levelled by Marino against Pietrostefani – of being one of the instigators of the murder of Calabresi? Even in the case of Pietrostefani, however, elements of objective corroboration were found, and they were remarkable for their solidity. Here is one: Pietrostefani was seen, with Sofri, in the Rome office of the newspaper *Lotta Continua*, on the morning of Calabresi's murder, 'anxiously awaiting' news. According to whom? According to Marino, of course. Here is another: 'The presence – certainly not claimed to have been constant – in Turin of Pietrostefani in the years 1971 and 1972 and his meetings with Marino in the home of the married couple Buffo–Paravia . . .' (Fifth Section, p. 17). According to the Court of Appeal (verdict [ii]), the frequent meetings between Pietrostefani and Marino in the years 1971 and 1972 supposedly proved that Pietrostefani had incited Marino to kill Calabresi – a form of reasoning in which the United Sections had detected '*a logical fault* per se *sufficient to invalidate the verdict of the Milanese court*' (SU, p. 92). In verdict (vi), the earlier years of Pietrostefani were again brought up, but in another context, adopted by the Fifth Section. Antonia Bistolfi, consort of Leonardo Marino, stated that she had never seen Pietrostefani 'take part in meetings of the movement in the Turin headquarters, nor perform any open activities on behalf of the organization in that city; hence the proper deduction that Pietrostefani must have been working for the clandestine structure in Turin . . .' (Fifth Section, p. 117). In other words, when the source of the accusation is not Leonardo Marino, it is Antonia Bistolfi. The United Sections had observed the remarkable parallelism between the two, observing that in order to verify the testimony of Marino it was necessary first of all to ascertain the credibility of his consort – who, among other things, had written mad, threatening letters to Adriano Sofri (SU, pp. 47–8). The Fifth Section, however, observed that the verdict of the trial before the Court of Appeal 'correctly confirmed the complete reliability' of the witness Bistolfi (Fifth Section, p. 117).

The 'proper deduction' based on the observations of Antonia Bistolfi is clearly entirely gratuitous. Concerning the existence and the purposes of a clandestine structure within Lotta Continua, the United Sections had already raised considerable doubt, contesting the statement in the appeals verdict (verdict [ii]) 'that this structure offered proof of the guilt of Sofri and Pietrostefani, entirely aside from the testimony of Marino' (SU, p. 49). Everything begins and ends with Marino (occasionally supported by the testimony of his consort, Bistolfi). Total proof – none.

8. Ovidio Bompressi – who, according to Marino's testimony, actually shot and killed Police Superintendent Calabresi, in the morning of the day of the crime – was in the town of Massa at one o'clock in the afternoon of the same day, working (according to the testimony, eighteen years later, of a number

of his friends, former Lotta Continua militants) to produce and distribute a flyer. In the verdict of the Court of Appeal (verdict [vi]) these witnesses were declared unreliable for a number of reasons. Special emphasis (noted the Fifth Section) was attributed:

> to the fact that eighteen years after the event it is practically impossible to remember something that is not tied to some other element of such importance that it *forces* recollection, and in the specific instance, the witnesses had 'remembered' only such substantially generic behaviour as the mimeographing of a flyer which was then to be distributed, but nothing that summoned to their memories the presence of Bompressi. (Fifth Section, p. 98)

This wordy statement conceals a banal tautology: we remember what we remember. Without disturbing the ghosts of Freud or Proust, everyone knows through direct experience that apparently meaningless events and details – which one would hardly expect to '*force* recollection' – are often etched into our memory. Still, it is another point that should be emphasized here. In the estimation of the Fifth Section, when Marino remembers events from sixteen years before, he is reliable; when Bompressi's friends are doing the remembering, they remember too much and are therefore unreliable. When, however, these same friends, or Police Superintendent Costantino, testify that they do not remember something which is definitely surprising, such as the alleged lightening of the colour of Bompressi's hair, there is no real problem: the Fifth Section imperturbably concludes that the 'slight lightening of the hair and the slight change in the hairdo, while moderately effective in eluding the notice of the law, certainly did not cause so great a change in appearance as to be noticed, and certainly not remembered eighteen years later' (Fifth Section, p. 101).

It was the witness Vigliardi Paravia, however, who had supposedly noticed the alleged lightening of the hair colour, making Bompressi look more like the Identikit of Calabresi's killer. As I explained (see above, pp. 67–68, 95–97), the question of the lightened hair probably derives from a confusion between the Identikit of the killer and the Identikit of the man who purchased the retractable umbrella found in the killers' car. In any case, Vigliardi Paravia's alleged comment, reported by Leonardo Marino and by his consort Antonia Bistolfi – and therefore requiring further documentation – was in any case a subjective evaluation, a comment: not evidence, not proof. However, the judges of the Fifth Section considered it to be precisely that.

The United Sections had declared that they could not accept a statement contained in the written judgement of the appeal trial (ii); specifically:

> that the particular nature of the crime that we are asked to ascertain also allows a different probatory consistency, whereby if the crime is by its very nature difficult to prove, then one will have to settle for evidence of lesser substance.... Nor is the matter settled by the argument that warns of the danger that grave guilt may remain unpunished, because this can and must lead us to sharpen the instruments that we use in our search for the truth, but it cannot lead us to ignore a benchmark in the development of judicial civilization. (SU, pp. 86–7)

The invitation to '*sharpen the instruments that we use in our search for the truth*' must sound – to anyone who has read this comment on the verdict of the Fifth Section – like a piece of involuntary irony. What sharpening of instruments? Adriano Sofri, Giorgio Pietrostefani and Ovidio Bompressi were sentenced to twenty-two years in prison *without a shred of proof*. The only evidence against them is the word of the 'repentant' (and the quote marks are obligatory) Leonardo Marino.

9. In the judgement of the second petition to the Court of Appeal of Milan (verdict [vi]), the standard mitigating circumstances were denied the three convicted killers, because – as the Fifth Section observed – of the 'complete absence of any signs of remorse, regret, or confession on the part of the defendants'.

This demand for 'remorse, regret, or confession' violates a basic human right – the right to proclaim and defend one's innocence. Sofri, Pietrostefani and Bompressi continue to proclaim their innocence. They did not flee, even though they could perfectly well have done so, since they all still possessed valid passports, right up until the final verdict. Pietrostefani was in France, and ran absolutely no risk of being extradited (in any case the murder had fallen under the statute of limitations); all the same, he joined his friends in prison, with a gesture denoting a truly great heart. All three indignantly refused, when it was suggested, to ask the President of the Italian Republic for a pardon. 'Only the guilty beg pardon,' Pietrostefani said. Human justice is fallible – why demand that a convicted killer feel remorse for a crime he may not have committed? Demands for repentance, remorse, confession and abjuration, however, come from another sort of tribunal – those of the Inquisition. The logic that led to the conviction of Bompressi, Sofri and Pietrostefani is the logic of the witch trial. Yet I would not wish to insist excessively on an analogy that conceals the dark, contemporary aspects of this affair. How can we interpret, for instance, the elimination by the police of elements of physical evidence? The vanishing of Calabresi's clothing; the sale at auction of the bullet that killed him; the destruction of the car used by the killers, 'because the road fund tax for the five-year period 1978–1983 remained unpaid', on 31 December 1988, when the preliminary inquest was already under way (see above, pp. 159–67) – should all these facts be attributed to mere imbecility? Only the naive, the ingenuous could think so. Let me not venture into the field of conjecture. What we have before us – consigned to the transcripts of the hearings and the seven verdicts – is enough, and more than enough. The trial of Sofri, Pietrostefani and Bompressi must be reopened. This shameful page in the history of Italian justice must be erased – and as soon as possible.

CHRONOLOGY

12 December 1969. At a crescendo in the labour conflicts of the 'hot autumn', four bomb blasts strike the Altar to the Fatherland, and the Banca Nazionale del Lavoro, in Rome, and the Banca Commerciale and the Banca dell'Agricoltura, in Milan. This last bank bombing killed seventeen people. Police, senior government figures, and the major press immediately proclaim, in chorus, the involvement of anarchists.

15 December 1969. An anarchist and railway employee named Pino Pinelli dies by falling from the window of the office of Police Superintendent Luigi Calabresi, on the fifth floor of the Milan police headquarters, where he had been detained for three days (in violation of the law). The police claim that Pinelli jumped out of the window, overwhelmed by the evidence implicating him and the anarchist Pietro Valpreda in the bombing. This version is immediately shown to be false. The episode causes enormous public feeling. Lotta Continua, in its daily paper, states that Pinelli was murdered and that the Italian state is implicated in the 12 December massacre.

1970. The Pinelli investigation is closed in May, then reopened – *de facto* – when Police Superintendent Calabresi sues the newspaper *Lotta Continua*, which has been accusing him for months, in articles and cartoons. The trial begins in October 1970, but is suspended the following April, when the court decides to order the exhumation of Pinelli's corpse for new tests; Calabresi's lawyer challenges the presiding judge, claiming that the judge has already stated in private that he is opposed to Calabresi.

Autumn 1971. Because of a complaint filed by Pinelli's widow, Licia, Calabresi and other officers and agents of the Milan police are charged with murder. The case is closed in October 1975 by Judge D'Ambrosio, who rules out both homicide and suicide, suggesting a theory of 'active illness'.

5 May 1972. In Pisa, on the eve of early political elections, there are violent battles between the police and youthful demonstrators summoned by Lotta Continua to block a rally by MSI, the Italian Neo-Fascist party. During the fighting a young anarchist, Franco Serantini, is beaten; he dies two days later in prison from the blows he suffered, and because he received no medical care.

17 May 1972. Calabresi is murdered in front of his residence, in the Via Cherubini in Milan, by two point-blank pistol shots. The first leads point to individuals linked to Lotta Continua. Over time, suspicion falls on a former Alfa Romeo factory worker who emigrated to Germany; two Irish militants, a man and a woman, guests in Italy of Lotta Continua; a young Milanese woman; and yet others.

31 May 1972.   At Peteano, near Gorizia, three *carabinieri* are killed in an ambush bombing. Senior *carabinieri* officers – who are later formally charged with attempting to mislead investigators (several are convicted) – announce the theory that the murder of Calabresi and the massacre at Peteano are both part of a single plot by Lotta Continua; they attribute this theory to the *pentito* Marco Pisetta.

17 May 1973.   During a ceremony for the inauguration of a commemorative bust of Police Superintendent Calabresi at Milan police headquarters, presided over by the Minister of the Interior, Mariano Rumor, Gianfranco Bertoli, a self-proclaimed 'individualist anarchist', tosses a hand grenade into the crowd, killing numerous innocent bystanders. Bertoli, who had already been in prison for eighteen years, on a life sentence without parole, emerges at the end of 1990 as a member of the Gladio organization. The intelligence services maintain that it is another person with the same name, while the magistrate who investigates finds that Bertoli's file is incomplete. Calabresi had begun to investigate Bertoli before he was killed. Following his murder, information on Bertoli and a photograph of him are sent by the Venice police to the Milan police, to show to the eyewitnesses to the murder, who fail to identify him.

1974.   Two right-wing extremists, the Milanese Gianni Nardi and the Roman Bruno Stefano, and a friend of theirs, Gudrun Kiess, a German woman, are charged with the murder of Calabresi. Nardi is accused of being the shooter, Kiess of driving the dark-blue Fiat 125 used in the killing. A few months later the two men are released when their alibi holds up; Kiess remains in prison for some time, despite the release of her fellow defendants and despite the fact that she has no driving licence.

November 1976. Lotta Continua disbands. For a few years, the newspaper continues publication.

1980. Prompted by rumours about former militants from the 'armed struggle', a Milanese member of Lotta Continua, Marco Fossati, comes under suspicion as the killer of Calabresi. Fossati learns that he is under suspicion from a headline and a photograph in a tabloid, describing him as the killer: the investigating magistrate, Lombardi, fails to notify him.

28 July 1988. Adriano Sofri, Giorgio Pietrostefani and Ovidio Bompressi are arrested at dawn in their homes, and transported to the *carabinieri* barracks in Milan. They are charged with having ordered (the first two) and committed (the third) the murder of Calabresi, on behalf of Lotta Continua. The charges are based on the accusations of Leonardo Marino who, in turn, claims that he drove the car used in the killing. Three months later, all three are released.

August 1989. Judge Lombardi completes the preliminary investigation, ordering a trial on charges of murdering Police Superintendent Calabresi for the four defendants, who – except for Sofri – are also charged with a series of armed robberies committed, according to Marino, between 1971 and 1973. Marino and other people he accuses are also charged with robberies committed up to 1987.

January 1990. The trial begins, in the Third Section of the Milan Court of Assizes. The court begins by dismissing the charges connected with the 'post-political' robberies, but includes the others. On 2 May 1990, after five days of deliberations, the court finds Sofri, Pietrostefani, Bompressi and Marino guilty of murder, sentencing the first three to twenty-two years in prison and Marino to eleven years. For the lesser crimes, a few of the defendants are acquitted, and in all cases the statute of limitations is applied. Sofri upholds his decision, announced prior to the trial, not to appeal. The Milan District Attorney's Office decides to delay his incarceration while his co-defendants appeal their convictions.

January 1991. Eight-and-a-half months after the verdict, the written judgement is submitted.

12 July 1991. The verdict is confirmed on appeal. The case of Sofri, who has refused to appeal, is joined with that of his friends.

23 October 1992. The United Penal Sections of the Supreme Court strike down the first verdict.

21 December 1993. Acquittal of all leading defendants. The written judgement, drawn up by an assessor who subscribes to the theory that the accused are guilty, induces the Supreme Court to strike down this verdict (27 October 1994).

11 November 1995. New verdict: the accused are guilty. Bompressi, Pietrostefani and Sofri are sentenced to twenty-two years in prison. Leonardo Marino, whose testimony constitutes the sole evidence for the prosecution, is acquitted for expiration of the statute of limitations. This verdict is upheld by the Fifth Penal Section of the Supreme Court on 22 January 1997.

24 January 1997. Bompressi and Sofri are locked up in prison in Pisa. Giorgio Pietrostefani – who has been living in France, where he was in no danger of extradition because French law would have argued expiration of the statute of limitations – decides to join his comrades, so that he can combine forces with them in the battle to clear their names. He leaves France on 29 January, and is subsequently sent to Pisa prison.